CONTEMPORARY SOUTHWESTERN JEWELRY

CONTEMPORARY
SOUTHWESTERN JEWELRY

DIANA F. PARDUE WITH THE HEARD MUSEUM

PHOTOGRAPHY BY CRAIG SMITH

Gibbs Smith, Publisher
TO ENRICH AND INSPIRE HUMANKIND
Salt Lake City | Charleston | Santa Fe | Santa Barbara

First Edition
11 10 09 08 07   5 4 3 2 1

To Mareen Allen Nichols

Published by
Gibbs Smith, Publisher
P.O. Box 667
Layton, Utah 84041

Orders: 1.800.835.4993
www.gibbs-smith.com

Designed by Kurt Hauser
Printed and bound in China

Library of Congress Cataloging-in-Publication Data

Pardue, Diana F.
   Contemporary Southwestern jewelry / Diana Pardue.—1st ed.
      p. cm.
   Includes bibliographical references.
   ISBN-13: 978-1-4236-0190-6
   ISBN-10: 1-4236-0190-4
   1. Indians of North America—Jewelry—Southwest, New. 2.
Indian silverwork—Southwest, New. 3. Turquoise jewelry—
Southwest, New. I. Title.

E78.S7.P36 2007
739.27089'97079—dc22

                        2006102582

Cover photo:
Charlene Reano detail of mosaic
necklace, 2006.

This page:
Veronica Poblano earrings of drusy
garnet, drusy cobalt calcite, and silver, 2005.

CONTENTS

7   Introduction
9   Acknowledgments

11   **A New Era, A New Direction**

29   **Metalwork**
      Modern Jewelry Design and Creation
      Casting
      Fabrication
      Doming
      Stamp Work
      Repoussé
      Texturing the Metal
      Appliqué
      Overlay

99   **Stone Patterning**
      Emphasizing the Metal and Stonework
      Mosaic on Shell or Wood
      Stone Inlay
      Carving in Stone and Shell
      Bead Necklaces

139   **Emerging Artists**
      Contemporary Jewelry Today
      Epilogue

178   Notes
180   Photo Credits
180   Jewelry Collection Credits
181   Bibliography
182   Index

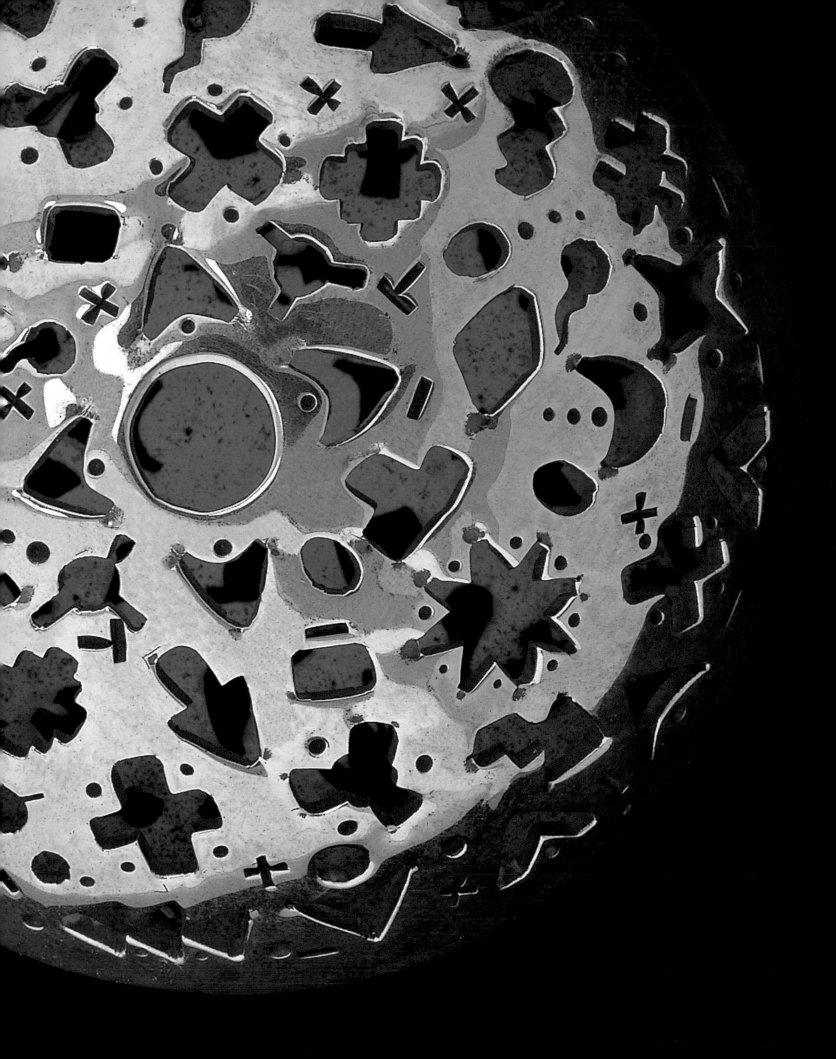

INTRODUCTION

Over the past fifty years, American Indian contemporary jewelry has transformed from a regional style to an art form of international acclaim. The enthusiastic response to Charles Loloma's jewelry in the 1970s and 1980s by collectors in France, Germany, and other European venues was an initial step toward firmly positioning American Indian jewelry within a world market. The incorporation of Southwestern jewelry with couture by clothiers such as Saks Fifth Avenue and fashion designers such as Ralph Lauren, also in the 1970s, brought attention to the changing art form. All of these factors combined with individual creativity to have an indelible impact on contemporary jewelry.

This book features the creations of several accomplished contemporary jewelers and is organized in distinct categories according to the techniques the artists use to transform a concept into a work of art. Although today's artists may have experimented with diverse techniques and have become accomplished in several, they choose specific methods to create jewelry in their unique style. Each section in this book highlights examples of a particular technique, even if the jewelry incorporates multiple ones. The driving force behind this book was to illustrate exceptional examples in these diverse technical areas rather than to select a set number of artists and a set number of photographed works per artist.

The book includes jewelry by artists who live and work in the Southwest, even though some were born in other regions. Many artists from areas outside of the Southwest have been in the Santa Fe area for decades, and their contributions to contemporary jewelry are significant. The jewelry featured here reflects different artistic experiences that for some include research and studies of jewelry from their culture, while others were influenced by university studies or an appreciation of jewelry or other art forms from other countries.

The silverwork included is not limited to wearable forms but includes containers of many different shapes based on diverse concepts. Small tobacco canteens were some of the earliest functional objects made in copper and silver. Over the past century, cigarette boxes, spoons and forks, napkin rings, punch bowls, teapots, and other functional shapes have also been made. Silversmiths have used a variety of metal fabrication techniques to create challenging shapes. Containers have been appreciated by collectors for elements of beauty rather than function. An appreciation for form and beauty has also served as collecting criteria for the small seed pots made by Norbert Peshlakai and others. Containers of many shapes, some without function, are included in this book. They exhibit the conceptual ingenuity of individual artists and at times may also display subtle humor. Containers constitute a substantial number of works in metal made today, and their jewel-like qualities have placed them in this book along with wearable art forms.

ACKNOWLEDGMENTS

Many people have helped bring this project to fruition. Heard Museum staff photographer Craig Smith, who took extraordinary care with each photograph, is deserving of particular recognition. Heard Museum director, Frank Goodyear, and director of collections, education, and interpretation, Ann Marshall, were supportive of the project. Other staff members who offered encouragement include Joe Baker, LaRee Bates, Kristen Caughlin, Kevin Coochwytewa, Larissa Curtis, Tricia Loscher, Bruce McGee, Sharon Moore, Patsy Stewart, and Marie Wittwer. Many jewelry enthusiasts were also helpful. They include JoAnn and Robert Balzer, Elizabeth Boeckman, Mary Cavanaugh, Carol Cohen, Fran Dickman, Diana Douglass, Andy Eisenberg, Bill Faust, Helen Gabriel, Hal and Margaret Gates, Carol Gunn, Jeanie Harlan, Lanny Hecker and Mavis Shure, Jan Hendler, Kathleen L. Howard, Anne Kern, Helen Kersting, Charles King, Sara Lieberman, Joy and Don McCann, J. L. Pete and Sara Morgan, Gary, Brenda and Harrison Ruttenberg, Vicki Samson, Marlene Scholsohn, Philip Smith, Martha Struever, Austin and Daune Turner, and Gene Waddell. I would also like to thank *American Indian Art* magazine and the Albuquerque International Sunport. Additionally, I would like to extend a special note of thanks to Marcia and Bill Berman and Deborah Slaney. It was my pleasure to work with Katie Newbold, project editor for this book.

This book draws extensively but not exclusively from the collections of the Heard Museum and from jewelry featured in the Heard Museum Shop. Additionally, a small number of silver and gold containers from two distinctive collections were featured in this publication. Fred and Helen Spielman began collecting silver containers in 1993 and have subsequently developed an extensive collection. They seek quality containers with the caveat that each has a lid, whether it is hinged or separate from the base. The Spielmans generously allowed several examples from their collection to be included in this book. Norman Sandfield has been collecting silver seed jars for more than twenty years. He purchased his first by Norbert Peshlakai from Martha Struever at her gallery in Chicago. In 2005 and 2006, Norman donated a collection of 172 silver seed jars to the Heard Museum, and by spring 2007, he had collected an additional seventy jars, bringing his total collection to 240. A small selection is featured here, and the collection is the subject of an extensive book, *Old Traditions in New Pots: Silver Seed Pots from the Norman L. Sandfield Collection*, written by Tricia Loscher.

I am also indebted to Martha Struever and the Wheelwright Museum staff for their exhibit and publication *Loloma: Beauty Is His Name,* which provides an in-depth overview of Charles Loloma's life and work. During the time the "Loloma" exhibit was shown at the Heard Museum, other works by Charles Loloma were brought to the attention of the Heard staff, which gave us the opportunity to photograph the jewelry and include it in this publication.

I am grateful to the artists whose works are included in this book, many of whom offered suggestions of their work for inclusion. Also, whenever possible, I provided the artists the brief biographical sketches I had written about them, and they were kind enough to correct misinterpreted facts that appeared in previously published articles or information that I had misunderstood in conversations or interviews. It is my hope that the biographical sketches, although brief, provide insight into the creative process.

A NEW ERA, A NEW DIRECTION

American Indian jewelry has long been recognized for its creativity and experimentation. Native jewelers have emphasized the beauty of natural forms and have been willing to use new materials. Several jewelers, including Hopi jeweler Charles Loloma, Navajo silversmith Kenneth Begay, Mexican/Mission jeweler Preston Monongye, and others, have been recognized for contemporary innovations. Loloma is perhaps the best-known and most widely recognized jeweler for his use of varied materials and techniques. He, more than any other individual, changed the face of contemporary Native American jewelry.[1] Loloma transformed traditional techniques such as tufa-casting, a method that uses a volcanic stone as a mold for metal, by leaving surfaces rough after casting rather than polishing them to a sheen as artists before him had routinely done. Loloma also introduced new stones to Native American jewelry such as lapis lazuli, malachite, and charoite, which he combined with wood and fossilized ivory that he inlaid in complex patterns reminiscent of the rugged mesa tops of his home in northern Arizona. As Loloma's innovative designs became accepted within the constraints that surrounded Native American jewelry, it became possible for the next generation of jewelers, many of whom are now accomplished in the field, to undertake varied avenues of design or techniques without restriction.

No one factor or event can explain the efforts and innovations of Begay, Loloma, and other artists working in Scottsdale, Arizona, in the 1950s and 1960s. It is intriguing to examine the town that fostered so many notable jewelers that also included Pala Mission artist Larry Golsh, Navajo artists James Little, Jesse Monongya, and Harvey Begay, and Hopi jeweler Charles Supplee. Similarly, in Santa Fe, New Mexico, in the late 1970s, Yazzie Johnson and Gail Bird, Richard Chavez, and Norbert Peshlakai began to initiate new and exciting changes in jewelry and metalwork.

The environment that fostered mid-century arts and artists in Arizona grew from a complexity of factors that included a decades-old appreciation of American Indian art, a post–World War II development of artist colonies, and an increasing migration of inhabitants to the Valley of the Sun. As the 1950s approached, Scottsdale burst on the scene. Begun in the early 1900s like other Arizona cities, Scottsdale's initial growth was based on an influx of people seeking a dry climate to assist in the alleviation of various lung disorders that included asthma and consumption, more acidulously known as tuberculosis. Aided by the development and accessibility of air conditioning in the 1950s and canal irrigation, the desert town once frequented only during the winter months by Easterners fleeing cold climates and seeking sunny resort locations became suitable for people who wanted to inhabit the area year-round.

Scottsdale, Phoenix, and other neighboring cities in the Valley of the Sun have long and diverse histories as resort destination points. Many of the cities also had shops that sold American Indian cultural arts. Some of the resorts also contained shops, which were often located in or near the lobbies that sold American Indian arts and crafts. An early example is the San Marcos Resort, which opened in Chandler in 1913. A shop that sold American Indian cultural arts, particularly baskets, was located in the complex of the San Marcos resort and was managed by Anna Fullen Croft (later Anna Fullen Smith) from 1925 through 1930. In Phoenix, the Arizona Biltmore—the only hotel with a Frank Lloyd Wright–influenced design— was completed in 1929. Wright's former student Albert Chase McArthur designed it in collaboration with Wright. That same year the Westward Ho opened in downtown Phoenix and the Wigwam opened in Litchfield.

Wright, along with several artists who settled in Scottsdale, enhanced the city's reputation as an artist colony. Many artists, such as local painter Phillip Curtis, had moved to the Scottsdale area during the Depression, and their creative works were primarily funded through the Works Progress Administration, a federal program that provided income for arts projects or to arts teachers. Wright formed a unique artist enclave in 1937 when he bought six hundred acres in Scottsdale and began to build, with the help of young emerging architects, Taliesin West, a center for architects that continues today.

In the past, ancestral peoples used local stones such as turquoise and jet along with trade items such as coral and shells to fashion elegant items of adornment. Turquoise was ground and shaped into beads for necklaces or cut into small pieces adhered to shells in mosaic patterns for use as pendants or bracelets. Shells were also acid-etched using fermented fruit of the saguaro cactus to form designs used in various jewelry items. Stone and shells were also cut, shaped by grinding by hand on local sandstone, and polished to form beads. These decorative items formed the basis and legacy of American Indian jewelry and continue to influence some contemporary jewelers today.

The 1950s brought Kenneth Begay and his cousins Allan and George Kee to Scottsdale through their working association with John Bonnell, owner of the White Hogan.[2] Bonnell moved his American Indian art business to Scottsdale from Flagstaff and established it on First Avenue west of Scottsdale Road, where the business remained until September 2006. The White Hogan distinguished itself through the sale of quality service ware—silver tea and coffee service, serving spoons, aperitifs—many of which combined sterling silver with Arizona ironwood, a novelty that continues to delight and intrigue collectors today. It was an atmosphere that fostered creativity through the works of Begay, the Kee brothers, and Begay's brother Johnnie Mike. For years, these four talented jewelers would win awards at local competitions at the Heard Museum Fair, the Arts and Crafts Exhibit, also held at the Heard Museum, and the Scottsdale National.

Another important business established in Scottsdale was that of Cherokee artist and scholar Lloyd Kiva New. A graduate of the School of the Art Institute, Chicago, New taught art at the Phoenix Indian School, a boarding school with grounds that stretched from Central Avenue to Seventh Street, north of Indian School Road. The school drew American Indian students from diverse backgrounds, and New had been asked to arrange for a mural to be painted at the 1939 Golden Gate International Exposition in San Francisco. Hopi painter Fred Kabotie was one of the muralists, and he recommended a young Hopi artist, Charles Loloma, to assist in painting the mural.[3] Twenty-two-year-old New's meeting with seventeen-year-old Loloma would be fortuitous for both men and ultimately for American Indian jewelry.

After two years of teaching at the Phoenix Indian School, New left to serve in the U.S. Navy during World War II, and he later returned to Scottsdale to begin a fashion design business. In 1946, his first store was on Brown and Main in Scottsdale in a building that had been an old grocery store. There, New worked as a designer to produce his line of clothing and handbags. Loloma and his wife, Otellie, joined New in 1956. The couple had studied formal ceramic techniques at the School for American Craftsmen at Alfred University from 1947 to 1949, after which they moved back to Hopi where they both taught at Second Mesa Day School.[4]

Scottsdale continued to develop its identity. Promoted by the city council as the "West's Most Western Town," the city adopted western architecture fashioned after a Hollywood stage set of the old west, complete with clapboard buildings and saloon-inspired pubs like the Pink Pony that had hitching posts along the dirt streets. The city was rapidly becoming an arts colony and a tourist destination point that provided a unique visitor experience.[5]

The Arizona Craftsmen building, with its open studios, initially began in a farmer's market and icehouse on the corner of Brown and Main Streets. The emphasis on handmade arts and crafts at the Craft Center fit the image the city fathers were promoting. In 1950, after a fire decimated the building, many of the artists moved north to agricultural land east of Scottsdale Road and south of the canal to wood frame buildings. New and several of the artists, including fashion designers Leona Caldwell and Maryon Johnson, and jewelers John

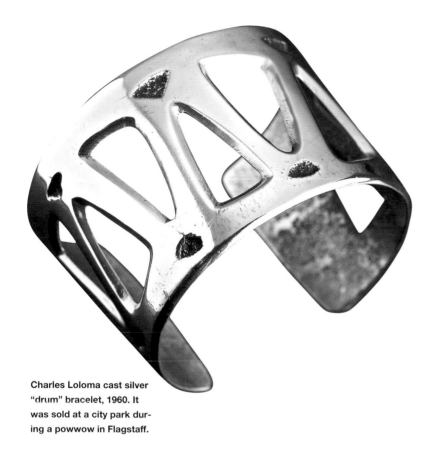

Charles Loloma cast silver "drum" bracelet, 1960. It was sold at a city park during a powwow in Flagstaff.

Charles Loloma cast silver bowguard inlaid with turquoise and coral, 1968.

D. Stanton and H. Fred Skaggs, moved to a final location at Fifth Avenue, called it the Arizona Craftsman Center, and opened it in 1956.[6]

New began creating handmade silk-screened fabrics and designing clothing and leather handbags, one of which was purchased by former first lady Eleanor Roosevelt. Creative expression was paramount to New, who talked about his work in 2001. He stated, "The freedom to express should not be hindered by ideas that Indians did the best work they could do in 1890." His friend and former colleague painter Fritz Scholder said of New that he "merged Indian symbols with contemporary Anglo concepts."[7] The Fifth Avenue location eventually featured annual fashion shows that included a 500-foot ramp for the models to display local couture. Loloma, although reportedly a potter, was also making jewelry while working at the craft center. It is not known if he took jewelry classes at Alfred, where he and Otellie had access to Manhattan museums and galleries, but soon Loloma was designing buttons for New's clothing line as well as pendants for the handbags.[8]

Loloma distinguished his jewelry early in his career through unusual interpretations of metalwork techniques, designs, and applications of stones. Loloma often used tufa casting to shape his silver jewelry, leaving large surface areas rough and unpolished. One sterling silver bracelet was referred to by Loloma as a "drum" bracelet when he sold it at a powwow at the Flagstaff city park around 1960. The bracelet design looks like the taut strings that secure the head of the drum. The surface is highly polished with small areas left rough, a method that Loloma would frequently reverse, leaving large areas rough and unpolished. This technique was quite different for its time, but he applied it to many types of jewelry, including necklaces, earrings, bracelets, buckles, bolo ties, and bowguards. A silver bowguard made by Loloma in 1968 has one side rough and unpolished and another highly polished. These two sections are di-

vided by a band of inlaid turquoise and coral.

Early bracelets were varied and experimental, and Loloma applied techniques, designs, and concepts that were unique to American Indian and mainstream jewelry. For one unusual bracelet made around 1958–59 and sold at the Kiva Craft Center, Loloma used sheet silver to fabricate the band rather than casting it—the technique for which Loloma would become so well known. The decorative element appliquéd to the band, however, was of cast silver.

The shape of the cast decoration is one that Loloma would vary later for other jewelry forms, including one earring in an unmatched pair made in 1960. The decorative element on the bracelet has a pink spinel or tourmaline in the center, and the similarly shaped decorative earring has amber. Also, each of the cast motifs that surrounds the stones consists of a design of radiating lines ending in silver drops. The creation of unmatched earrings was revolutionary for American Indian jewelry, and the use of amber was not at all traditional. Loloma would transform the concept of unmatched earring sets later when he would introduce the concept of

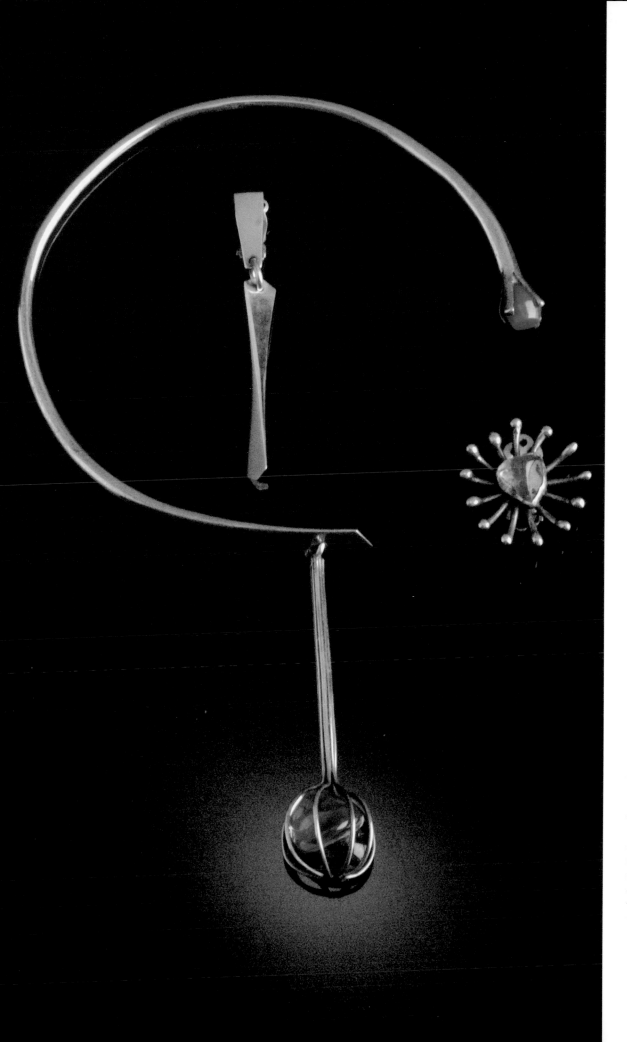

Above: Charles Loloma designed a concept of a single earring, mainly of turquoise beads but often including coral and other stones. The inspiration was historic turquoise bead earrings worn in pairs. This earring was made of turquoise, ironwood, and 14k gold, 1969.

single earrings.

Around the time Loloma made the unmatched earring sets, he also began to inlay patterns of stones in bracelets, on bolo ties, and in cufflinks. One inlaid bracelet made in 1966 has silver cones attached. A letter opener made in 1959 illustrates Loloma's early application of inlay stones that include turquoise, coral, and wood inset in a linear pattern on the handle.

Loloma was initially known in Phoenix and Scottsdale for his pottery. In 1959, the Heard Museum published a photograph of Loloma with an announcement stating "Charles Loloma will demonstrate Hopi pottery making at the First Annual Fair."[9] Although the announcement indicates that Loloma would demonstrate pottery, the photo shows him holding a tufa mold, a natural volcanic rock carved for the purpose of casting molten metal to make jewelry. He may have been known for his pottery at this time, but within a few years he would be better known for his jewelry. The Heard Fair was held on Saturday, May 23, from 11:00 a.m. to 10:00 p.m. and Sunday, May 24, from 11:00 to 7:00 p.m. Through the leadership of the Heard Museum board of trustees, the museum's volunteer organization called the Heard Museum Guild, and curator H. Thomas Cain, the fair brought American Indian jewelry, pottery, textiles, and other arts, native foods, and performances to the attention of visitors. For the Heard, this was a small step in artist participation that would grow to an annual event that today features more than 650 artists.

Jolted by the heat but fueled with a good idea, by 1961, the Third Annual Heard Fair was held in the much cooler month of March. It was open Saturday and Sunday, March 25–26, from 10:00 a.m. to 6:00 p.m. daily. The chairperson for the event was Mrs. Dean (Mareen) Nichols, who would become an avid collector of contemporary southwestern jewelry including more than twenty examples made by Charles Loloma. The addition of air conditioning that year alleviated concerns for any excessive heat waves. Within the two years since the first Heard Museum Fair, Charles Loloma had established his career as a jeweler and was acknowledged in the local newspaper announcement

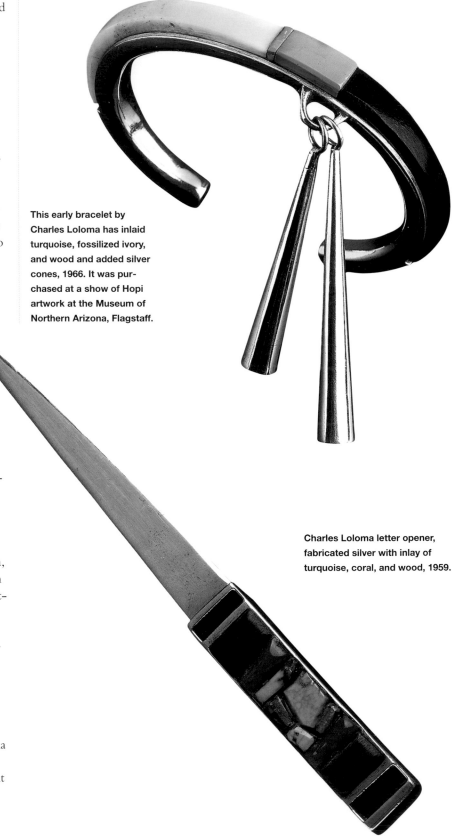

This early bracelet by Charles Loloma has inlaid turquoise, fossilized ivory, and wood and added silver cones, 1966. It was purchased at a show of Hopi artwork at the Museum of Northern Arizona, Flagstaff.

Charles Loloma letter opener, fabricated silver with inlay of turquoise, coral, and wood, 1959.

This photograph of Lloyd Kiva New and Charles Loloma (right) appeared in an article in the *Scottsdale Progress* about an arts event that featured the work of students from the Institute of American Indian Art held at the Heard Museum in January 1964.

Charles Loloma holds a tufa mold in a photograph advertising the Heard Museum First Annual Fair in 1959.

for the fair stating "The Charles Lolomas of Scottsdale will demonstrate and display their unusual and original jewelry." The article also noted that "the Museum shop will sell authentic Indian jewelry."[10]

In 1962, the Fourth Annual Heard Fair was held Saturday, March 24, beginning at 10:00 a.m. and Sunday, March 25, beginning at noon and continuing each day until sundown. The fair chairperson was Mrs. Jack Ross, a former model and Hollywood actress, whose stage name was Aquanetta and whose movies included *Tarzan and the Leopard Woman*. Aquanetta, a local celebrity, actively attended Heard Museum events through the 1970s, and her photograph with Navajo painter Andrew Tsinajinnie was featured in the article promoting the Heard's fourth fair. The article confirmed that "jewelers Charles and Otellie Loloma

will be at the Fair."[11] By 1962, Charles Loloma was firmly established in Scottsdale and Phoenix as a Native American jeweler with jewelry available and on view for the reported thousands of visitors who attended the Heard Museum fair that year.

That same year, Lloyd Kiva New fulfilled a lifelong dream to establish a national Indian art school when he agreed to serve as director of arts for the burgeoning Institute of American Indian Arts in Santa Fe. New and Charles Loloma had directed the activities at the Southwest Indian Art Project sponsored by the Rockefeller Foundation and held at the University of Arizona in Tucson in the summers of 1960 and 1961.[12] Inspired by the enthusiasm generated by the project and with a strong background in teaching, Charles and Otellie Loloma were among the first instructors hired at the institute that would have a distinguished staff that included Apache sculptor Allan Houser and young Luiseño Mission painter Fritz Scholder. Charles Loloma became director of the plastic arts department at the Institute. Loloma, who was generous with his knowledge, taught Fritz Scholder how to make jewelry, which Scholder reportedly did until his paintings began to sell.[13]

Both New and Loloma maintained close ties to Arizona and to the Heard Museum. In January 1964, they returned to the Heard for an arts event that showcased student works in the fields of art, music, and poetry. New provided a lecture, students enacted an original drama, and actor Vincent Price read student poetry. Accompanying this was an exhibit of student works, which was set up by Charles Loloma, "who teaches jewelry and merchandizing" at the Institute.[14]

After a few short years of teaching at the Institute, Loloma returned to the Hopi village of Hotevilla, where he established his studio. Loloma also sold jewelry to several galleries including the Heard Museum Shop, which was managed by gallerist Lovena Ohl. In December 1971, Loloma had his first one-man exhibit at the museum. He was experimenting with lost wax casting and continuing to explore the application of materials not typically used by Southwest jewelers, such as pearls. Loloma chose not only traditional spherical cultured pearls but also baroque pearls with their unusual shapes and colors. Some of his lost wax–cast designs,

with an article about Al Momaday written by esteemed art instructor Dorothy Dunn. Dunn had established herself as the premier instructor of such talented painters as Fred Kabotie, Allan Houser, Geronima Montoya, and others when she taught painting at the Santa Fe Indian School from 1932 to 1962.

New Mexico Magazine's March/April 1970 issue had a photograph of the young, talented, and photogenic painter Helen Hardin with a feature story about her work. Hardin had participated in the Rockefeller Foundation–sponsored workshop and arts classes at the University of Arizona along with Navajo painter Mary Morez and Hopi artist Michael Kabotie, who would develop his skills not only as a talented painter but also as a skilled jeweler.

It was a full year before the magazine would feature another painter, the young R. C. Gorman, followed by Fritz Scholder in the May/June issue of the same year. Indian art met Hollywood with the use of the provocative pop culture title "Will Success Spoil Fritz Scholder?" which was derived from the title of the 1957 feature film *Will Success Spoil Rock Hunter?* starring Tony Randall and Jayne Mansfield. *Arizona Highways* shifted the emphasis toward painters in the September 1972 issue with an article about Diane O'Leary.

In December 1971, a one-person sales exhibit was held for Charles Loloma at the Heard Museum in Phoenix. Loloma had been making jewelry for more than twenty years and was fifty years old when he had his first one-man show at the Heard. Seven years later, in 1978, the retrospective show at the Heard featured his work and included a broad range of jewelry that exhibited innovative techniques and designs. He would continue to develop others over the next few years. The generations of jewelers that followed were influenced by his work and many of them directly attribute design ideas or techniques to Loloma. When Loloma began making jewelry, squash blossom necklaces, concho belts, and bolo ties (the official neckwear of Arizona) were bountiful. Turquoise was plentiful in rich and varied colors of blue and blue green, as turquoise mines in Arizona, New Mexico, Colorado, and Nevada provided ample quality stones for use in jewelry.

Not bound by the obligation to show only the work of artists within a particular state, like *Arizona Highways* and *New Mexico Magazine*, the Heard Museum was developing an emphasis on contemporary regional arts and was free to show the work of Helen Hardin, Fritz Scholder, R. C. Gorman, Mary Morez, and Allan Houser. In a series of contemporary shows, all of which were sales shows, the Heard exhibited the work of these painters and sculptors and other artists, such as potter Tony Da and Charles Loloma.

Nationwide attention was focused upon American Indian art in the 1970s as fashion designers Ralph Lauren and Calvin Klein incorporated American Indian designs into their couture. During those years, the Heard Museum held annual juried invitational arts and crafts sales shows. People arrived early in the day and brought lawn chairs, which they placed near the Monte Vista Street entrance of the museum to stake out their position to be first in line to rush into the gallery and purchase prize-winning works of art. Visitors could not preview the artwork until the day of the event. Esteemed artists Allan Houser, Charles Loloma, Tony Da, and Al Momaday were judges for the 1972 Arts and Crafts show. The prize-winning work in silver was a large platter with stamped designs of Yei figures made by Kenneth Begay, which Charles Loloma held for a photograph on the day of the juried competition.

Arizona Highways and *New Mexico Magazine* continued to feature American Indian art, occasionally turning their attention to jewelry. In an unprecedented move, *Arizona Highways* included an article written by an American Indian artist in the June 1972 issue. Mission/Mexican and adopted Hopi jeweler Preston Monongye titled his article "The New Indian Jewelry Art of the Southwest." Charles Loloma's jewelry was pictured, as was Monongye's. For the next issue of *Arizona Highways*, Monongye wrote another article about the Gallup Inter-tribal Ceremonial titled "After 51 Miracles."

Similarly, *New Mexico Magazine*'s July/August 1973 issue included an article titled "The Romance of Indian Jewelry," although much of the jewelry featured was more traditional in scope. Perhaps the most innovative article in terms of its intent to feature Indian fashion and jewelry was an article in the November/December 1973 issue of *New Mexi-*

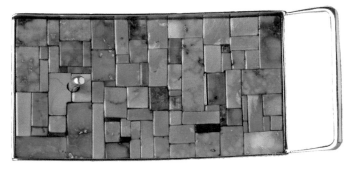

Above and right: Charles Loloma fabricated 14k gold buckle with inlaid lapis lazuli and coral, and on the reverse side inlaid turquoise, coral, and lapis lazuli, 1975.

Below, left: From left: Heard Museum Arts and Crafts Exhibit judges Al Momaday, Fred Kabotie, Allan Houser, Charles Loloma, and Tony Da, 1972.

Below, right: Charles Loloma holds a first-prize-winning silver platter with stamped designs by Kenneth Begay at Heard Museum Arts and Crafts Exhibit in 1972.

co Magazine. Titled "Red is Chic," the article featured contemporary American Indian–designed fashion by Carol Tsosie and Ramoncita Sandoval. One model was Helen Hardin, who wore jewelry by Preston Monongye and Lee and Mary Yazzie. After those early years of showing work by leading contemporary painters, *New Mexico Magazine* settled into a pattern of including articles about more traditional works, beginning with the May/June 1974 issue, which had a 1932 jar by Maria Martinez on the cover. In contrast, *Arizona Highways* showed work by cutting-edge contemporary artists such as that of Martinez's grandson, Tony Da. *Arizona Highways* reflected the glitz and glamour of Scottsdale.

The national interest in American Indian art was reflected in the contents of the two magazines. By the release of the September/October 1974 issue of *New Mexico Magazine*, a full-page advertisement on the inside cover informed readers that the copies of the May/June issue with Maria Martinez pottery on the cover were no longer available. In 1975, the magazine, which transitioned to a monthly publication, reprinted the Martinez article and combined it with the January/February 1974 article "The Romance of Navajo Weaving" and the March 1975 "Kachina Special" article. The magazine advertised the trio of Indian arts articles on the back covers of the June through September 1975 issues and other issues into 1976.

In 1974, three issues of *Arizona Highways* featured contemporary jewelry, pottery, and textiles. The magazine started the year with the January issue devoted to turquoise and included a photograph of Charles Loloma jewelry. February featured ancestral pottery, but the May issue returned to the contemporary format with an article titled "Dreams in Clay, Water and Fire," and the July issue had contemporary Navajo weavings, including photographs of prize-winning textiles from the collection of Phoenix businessman Read Mullan that would later be donated to the Heard. The pinnacle was the August issue that contained an article about Charles Loloma and his jewelry. In that same issue, Saks Fifth Avenue fashion was matched with contemporary American Indian jewelry. The photographs were interspersed, appearing in six pages of the issue. American Indian art themes continued

into the following years with jewelry again featured on the fiftieth anniversary issue in March 1975 and baskets in July 1975. All of these issues have become collectibles for Arizonians and others interested in American Indian art.

New Mexico Magazine continued to have articles about American Indian art in 1976, including "The Jewelry Traditions of Santo Domingo" in April and jewelry by Hopi artist Lewis Lomay in July. A new magazine, *American Indian Art Magazine*, was published in the autumn of 1975, and the inaugural issue included an article about Charles Loloma and his jewelry, featuring a photograph of two of his bracelets on the back cover. The next issue, Spring 1976, had a feature article about Larry Golsh and his jewelry and included a photograph of two bracelets on the cover. *American Indian Art Magazine* would quickly dominate the field of American Indian art, with *Arizona Highways* and *New Mexico Magazine* covering the subject matter occasionally. Of particular note is

Charles Loloma tufa-cast silver bracelet with an inlaid design of a snake in turquoise, fossilized ivory, wood, and coral, 1970s.

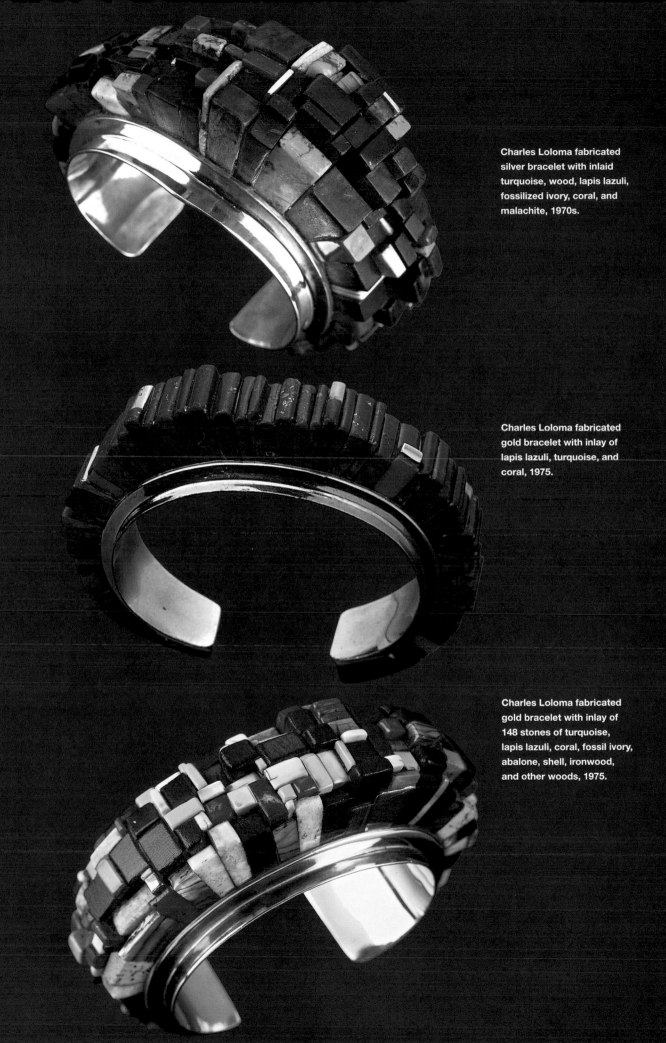

Charles Loloma fabricated silver bracelet with inlaid turquoise, wood, lapis lazuli, fossilized ivory, coral, and malachite, 1970s.

Charles Loloma fabricated gold bracelet with inlay of lapis lazuli, turquoise, and coral, 1975.

Charles Loloma fabricated gold bracelet with inlay of 148 stones of turquoise, lapis lazuli, coral, fossil ivory, abalone, shell, ironwood, and other woods, 1975.

Charles Loloma fabricated
silver bolo tie with inlaid
wood and turquoise, 1966.

Charles Loloma fabricated silver bolo tie with inlay of charoite, turquoise, coral, and lapis lazuli, 1980.

the April 1979 issue of *Arizona Highways*, which featured individual jewelers (and Santa Clara potter Nancy Youngblood modeling jewelry). On the back cover of this issue, models wear jewelry by Charles Loloma, Larry Golsh, and others against the backdrop of Monument Valley. The bracelet by Loloma featured in the issue has an inlay of 148 stones and wood. It was pictured in a double photograph that shows a side view of the bracelet over an enlarged view of the bracelet top.[17] Although Lois and Jerry Jacka produced five important articles for the magazine that included contemporary American Indian jewelry from May 1986 through October 1996, *Arizona Highways* did not feature jewelry on the cover again until the May 2003 issue.

By 1975, Charles Loloma was creating bracelets with various heights of inlay stones that reflected the jagged landscapes of mesa tops near his home. His use of materials such as lapis lazuli, fossil ivory, and malachite was non-traditional and dis-

tinguished his work. He would continue to incorporate new materials along with new designs. His intrigue with interesting stones and color patterning led him to select a mottled purple stone from Russia called charoite. It was another innovative step in his incorporation of unusual materials. Loloma also introduced new design concepts, creating corn maiden pendants of inlaid stones and in one instance carving the image in turquoise.

Contemporary jewelry had other venues. Martha Struever (then Hopkins) began showing Yazzie Johnson and Gail Bird's jewelry at the Indian Tree Gallery in Chicago as early as 1978, where she also featured jewelry by Charles Loloma. She quickly followed with the impressively stamped metalwork of the young Navajo jeweler Norbert Peshlakai, university-trained architect turned jeweler Richard Chavez from San Felipe, and others. In Santa Fe, the Dewey-Kofron Gallery featured Johnson and Bird's jewelry, including their thematic belts that incorporated myriad stones as well as their early garnet bead belts, of which they made only about six. Dewey Galleries also showed the silver seed jars that Norbert Peshlakai began to create in 1976, often embellishing extensively with stamp work created by silver stamping tools he also made.

Loloma influenced two generations of jewelers and paved the way for acceptance of contemporary designs and techniques. Although his initial entries in Native American competitions were rejected because the jewelry did not "look Indian," time and great creativity were on Loloma's side. As his work and the innovative work of others became accepted, contemporary jewelers had more latitude to develop creative ideas. Loloma's technique of adding a mosaic of stones on the interior of rings and bracelets inspired many artists. In the late 1970s, Yazzie Johnson and Gail Bird began creating designs on the reverse of buckles through the overlay technique, in which a design was cut out of a silver or gold plate of metal and laid above a solid plate of the same metal. They called the technique "underlay" because it was applied under the design. Other artists were experimenting and departing from the expected concepts of Indian jewelry. Larry Golsh, Yazzie Johnson, and Gail Bird were younger but were developing their jewelry at a time when Loloma was experimenting not only in design but also with diverse materials. Those artists and others benefited from Loloma's groundbreaking experiences as they developed their distinctive styles. Johnson and Bird incorporated picture jaspers and agates into thematic belts, but also placed them in necklaces in settings that were double sided, with the stone on one side and a design in overlay on the other. Other American Indian jewelers were observing Loloma's work and experimenting with casting. A young contemporary of Loloma's, Palo-

Mission artist Larry Golsh, said that he was so inspired by Loloma's work that he tried experimental casting on any surface, including rocks, but was most successful with cuttlefish bone casting.

In the 1950s, American Indian jewelry was forging a new path. Lloyd Kiva New's concept of freedom of expression was being fulfilled as jewelers selected from a range of metals, stones, and shells that could be used to express their imaginative and creative endeavors.

Charles Loloma at his 1971 opening at the Heard Museum.

Charles Loloma cufflinks with wood, turquoise, fossilized ivory, coral, and lapis lazuli, 1960s.

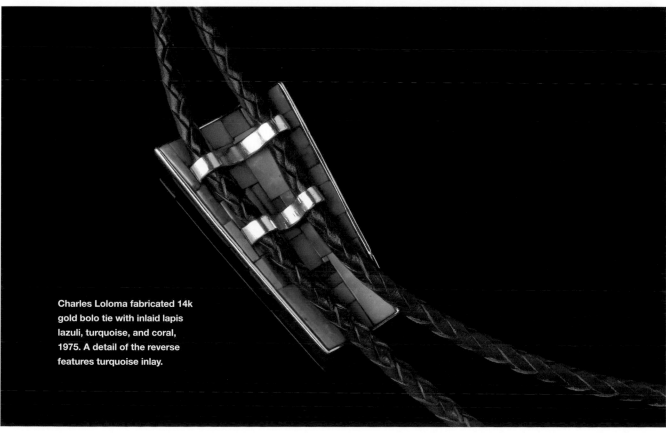

Charles Loloma fabricated 14k
gold bolo tie with inlaid lapis
lazuli, turquoise, and coral,
1975. A detail of the reverse
features turquoise inlay.

METALWORK

Modern Jewelry Design and Creation

A tremendous shift in southwestern jewelry designs and materials took place in the 1970s. Jewelers such as Kenneth Begay and Charles Loloma, whose entries were refused at American Indian art competitions, led the way for other young jewelers to experiment and move away from the expected forms in silver and turquoise, if they chose to do so. Those creations, still much appreciated for their classic beauty and clean lines, continue to be made and are highly sought after. Other jewelers now have the freedom to experiment, and their work appeals to a differ-ent clientele or collectors who favor both classic and experimental works.

Many of the same techniques used in jewelry making over one hundred years ago continue to be used today. Some are combined with techniques artists began to use after 1960, such as lost wax casting, cuttlefish bone casting, or setting precious stones, such as diamonds. Materials have also greatly changed. Kenneth Begay's use of ironwood in chess boards, teapot handles, and as decorative inlay in jewelry and other silver forms was a revolutionary step in American Indian jewelry and metalwork. Charles Loloma's incorporation of ironwood and other woods in inlay designs was innovative as

Preston Monongye tufa-cast silver bracelet with Royston turquoise, 1973.

well. The use of gold by Loloma and the generation of younger artists working in the 1970s created another dramatic change.

Artists continue to create unusual shapes or designs. Some use century-old techniques while others explore new ones. All of these concepts and ideas make up contemporary jewelry today. Each generation and each individual artist brings his or her design concepts to the art form, and they continue to introduce unusual materials to fully illustrate a concept.

Casting

Casting is a method of forming an object by heating metal, usually gold or silver, until it is molten and pouring it into or onto a prefabricated form to make that shape in metal once cooled. American Indian silversmiths have made casts from locally found volcanic rock or tuff since the late 1800s.[1] Mexican or American silver coins were preferred sources of silver until their use became prohibited. Some traders such as John Lorenzo Hubbell of Ganado, Arizona, provided coins to silversmiths until around 1890.[2]

The traditional method of tufa casting was used to make high profile shapes that were easier to accomplish by carving a deep design in a tufa stone that would hold the molten silver until it cooled and assumed the form of the mold. Bowguards, bracelets, and najas for necklaces were all traditionally made with this technique, although other techniques of fabricating silver could also be used to form these items. By 1950, American Indian silversmiths had been using tufa casting for more than seventy years without much alteration of the technique. Charles Loloma had just begun to experiment with the surface texture, allowing some areas of the rough-surfaced silver to go unpolished and, in the process, creating a contrast in textures that was innovative and offered a new look for contemporary jewelry.[3]

Other jewelers seeking new design concepts for contemporary works quickly followed Loloma's example. Preston Monongye (1927–87) created innovative designs in unpolished tufa-cast creations, often enhancing the design with turquoise, coral, shell, and other stones.

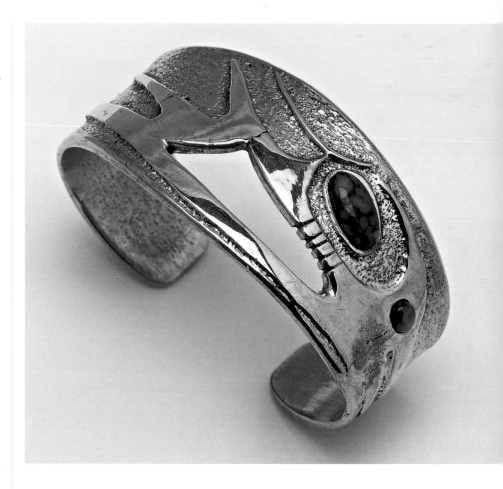

Monongye was a talented designer. Adopted by a Hopi family as a young boy, Monongye learned silver-making techniques by pumping the bellows to keep the fire going during jewelry making for his Hopi uncle David Monongye. As a young man, Monongye had a variety of jobs that included working at the Fred Harvey hotels and for trader Roman Hubbell, son of Ganado trader John Lorenzo Hubbell. Monongye also served in the U.S. Army in World War II and later worked for the Bureau of Indian Affairs.[4]

In the 1960s, Monongye decided to work with jewelry full time, initially making silver overlay in the style developed by the Hopi Guild. By 1966, like Charles Loloma, Monongye was leaving cast areas of his silver jewelry unpolished and was drawing inspiration for many designs from Hopi life and culture. That year, Monongye received the grand prize at the Gallup Inter-Tribal Ceremonial. Through the years, he would continue to receive

Preston Monongye tufa-cast 14k gold bracelet with Bisbee turquoise, 1975. Monongye was among an increasing number of American Indian artists who used gold instead of silver in the 1970s.

Jesse Monongya tufa-cast 18k gold buckle with diamonds, ruby, opal, and Candelaria turquoise, 2005. Jesse Monongya incorporates a design of a spider, an important figure in Navajo oral history, and a tufa-cast design of a web on this buckle. Monongya indicated that the large format of this buckle made it difficult to cast.

recognition and awards at Gallup, the Museum of Northern Arizona in Flagstaff, the Heard Museum Guild Arts and Crafts Exhibit, and the New Mexico State Fair. In 1970, Monongye won the grand prize at the Gallup Inter-Tribal Ceremonial for a tufa-cast container, the first fully cast container to be entered at the ceremonial.

Monongye often worked collaboratively with other jewelers, particularly Lee Yazzie and later his son Jesse Monongya, who inlaid the stones in the bracelets and other jewelry forms he designed. Monongye was also one of several Scottsdale-based artists who was a pioneer in using gold in American Indian jewelry.

In 1972, he received top awards at the Gallup Ceremonial and the New Mexico State Fair for a 14k gold–cast squash blossom necklace. His son, Jesse, developed keen lapidary skills in addition to his metalsmithing accomplishments.

Another jeweler experimenting with casting and innovative designs was Pala Mission artist Larry Golsh (b. 1942). Although Golsh grew up on the Pala Indian Reservation in California, his parents met at the Phoenix Indian School around 1940 where his grandmother worked. Golsh and his parents visited his grandmother frequently at the school, often staying for a month at a time. One of Golsh's earliest childhood memories is linked to the school's expansive grounds, which included a dairy, bakery, and hospital as well as employee housing. Golsh's parents were friends with Lloyd Kiva New, an instructor at the school, and his wife, Betty. Golsh remembers visiting with New in the art building and walking down hallways covered with murals that the Indian students had painted. Years later, when Golsh's mother took a job at the Phoenix Indian Hospital, Golsh continued to visit the school and art department. He recalls an environment where everybody knew everybody.

Golsh developed an interest in art while a student at North High School in Phoenix. He worked on the yearbook staff and took some photographs for the yearbook. A high school aptitude test revealed that he had a potential for engineering, architecture, and drafting in particular. Golsh visited Taliesen West around the same time and decided to study architecture at Arizona State University (ASU), where he also took art classes. While there, Golsh met sculptor and professor of art Ben Goo and decided to take sculpture classes. Golsh observed Goo's activities, which included teaching, sculpting, and entering works in the Arizona State Fair that won awards. Golsh switched his major from architecture to art.

During his freshman year at ASU in 1960, Golsh began to look for a part-time job. He went to the Lloyd Kiva New studio to talk with Betty New about potential jobs. She introduced him to Manfred Susunkewa, who worked designing and printing fabric. Golsh was hired to help Susunkewa, who is a recognized katsina doll carver today, make silkscreens and print the fabrics used in the shop at the Kiva Craft Center in Scottsdale. Golsh worked at the shop for two years.

Golsh recalls his first meeting with Charles Loloma at the Kiva Craft Center. "One afternoon, we hear a car screech up outside the studio. Here's this big guy driving a black Pontiac convertible with the top down and his hair was wild. It was Charles Loloma. He had been at the University of Arizona giving a talk. He and two girls were going up to Hopi and he had stopped by to see Manfred, who was Loloma's cousin."[5] Loloma extended an invitation to Golsh to visit him at his studio at Hopi.

Susunkewa had a jewelry bench in the studio at the Kiva Craft Center and had shown Golsh some basic silversmithing techniques—soldering, filing, and sawing shapes out of silver. Golsh later visited Loloma in his studio at Hotevilla and watched him work. Golsh admired Loloma's early work that emphasized the metalwork. While at his studio, Loloma showed him how to tufa cast, and Golsh was later shown the technique of lost wax casting by another jeweler in Phoenix.

Golsh had experience building models through his architecture studies at ASU, so he was well prepared for his next job while still at ASU, working for Italian architect Paolo Soleri, who had designed and was beginning to build a prototype city called Arcosanti, near Camp Verde, Arizona. Soleri was

Larry Golsh tufa-cast 18k gold bracelet with a design inspired by Mission basketry and 18k gold cuttlefish bone–cast ring with diamonds, 2004.

Larry Golsh 18k gold necklace with tufa-cast pen-
dants, 2002.

Larry Golsh coral bead
necklace with tufa-cast 18k
gold pendant with dia-
monds, 2004.

Larry Golsh coral bead
necklace with 18k gold
tufa-cast pendant and 18k
gold tufa-cast bracelet,
2005.

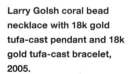

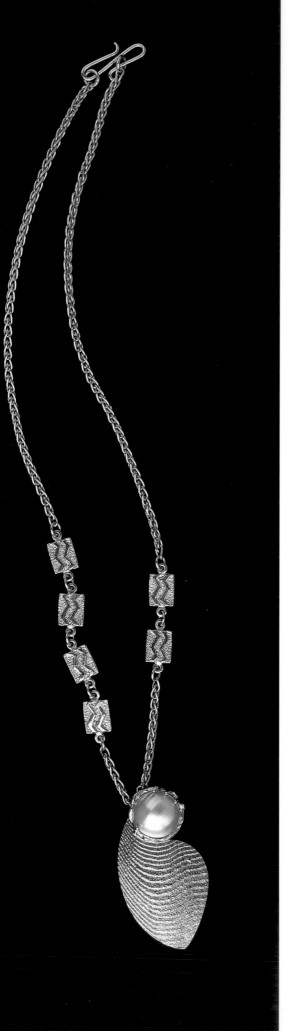

working on an exhibit titled "The Architectural Visions of Paolo Soleri," which incorporated architectural models and drawings. Golsh's work with the Paolo Soleri Architectural Exhibit took him to several museums nationwide, including the Cochran Gallery of Art in Washington, D.C., the Whitney Museum of American Art in New York, the Art Institute of Chicago, and the National Gallery of Art. Golsh traveled to help set up the exhibit installation of the Soleri show at the different museums and gave tours of the exhibit. He continued to make jewelry at Soleri's foundry between the museum exhibits.

Golsh continued to experiment with casting using a variety of surfaces that included wood and charcoal, as well as pouring wax on stone surfaces and then using the wax as a casting plate to achieve different textures. He noticed the technique of cuttlefish bone casting while looking through an old

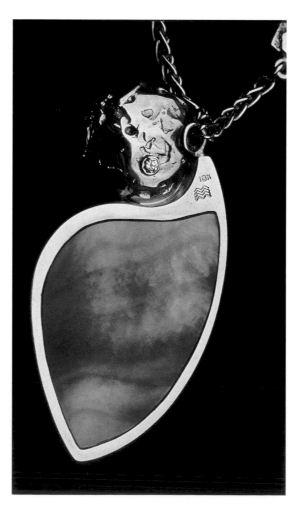

Larry Golsh 18k gold necklace, cuttlefish bone–cast pendant with mabe pearl, and tufa-cast satellites attached to chain, 1980s. Detail of pendant reverse with abalone and diamond.

Above, left: Harvey Begay 18k gold tufa-cast bracelet with coral, 1997.

Above, right: Harvey Begay 14k gold lost wax–cast bracelet with diamonds and lapis lazuli.

Right: Don Supplee 18k gold tufa-cast pendant with coral.

jewelry book and began to use that technique as a casting medium as well. Golsh became a leader among contemporary artists to use this technique. Golsh says, "I've always been an experimenter. I'm not afraid to try something new."[6]

In 1974, Golsh entered a few jewelry items in the Heard Museum Art and Crafts Exhibit and won several awards at the juried show. He met exhibit curator Jim Parker at the time and Parker introduced Golsh to Lovena Ohl, who was the manager of the Heard Museum Shop. Ohl asked Golsh for some jewelry to sell in the shop. When he responded that he did not have any additional works, she suggested that he go home and make something for the shop. In the flurry of the American Indian art craze of the 1970s, the Heard Museum show was prestigious, and Golsh credits winning awards at the show as being a boost to his career. Golsh continued to make sculptures, some of which were included in the 1973 "Sculpture I" and 1975 "Sculpture II" shows at the Heard Museum. At the latter, he was awarded a silver medal. In 1974, he was among eight noted artists whose works were included in the Heard Museum "Invitational '74." He also continued to make jewelry and work with Paolo Soleri.

In 1977, Lovena Ohl opened a shop near the

Ric Charlie tufa-cast silver and turquoise buckle, 1997. The colored palette is a technique Charlie developed by using liver of sulphur.

Civic Center in Scottsdale where she sold American Indian art, including Golsh's jewelry. She encouraged him to use only the best gem-quality turquoise, which was quite an expense for a beginning jeweler. Golsh met French jeweler Pierre Touraine at Ohl's shop. Touraine suggested that Golsh use diamonds in his work and offered to teach Golsh the necessary skills. Golsh set up a weekly schedule with Touraine where he learned lapidary skills and how to set precious stones, including diamonds. Golsh recalls that Touraine was always open to showing Golsh techniques or talking with him about designs or his own work, and Golsh credits Touraine as having a great influence on the quality of his jewelry.[7]

Working with Touraine provided Golsh an opportunity to blend European jewelry skills with American Indian concepts. Golsh focused on simple geometric forms with a contemporary touch, some of his creations being inspired by American Indian concepts and designs. The zigzag line that

Golsh often uses is derived from designs in Mission baskets made in California. Although baskets were not being made by the time Golsh was a boy, his grandmother had a number of basketry plaques in her home at Pala that Golsh admired.

Golsh entered his jewelry in several competitions, including the Scottsdale National. He was featured in Guy and Doris Monthan's pivotal book *Art and Indian Individualists* and was one of five artists featured in the 1984 Public Broadcasting Consortium series *American Indian Artists II.* Throughout his career he has favored tufa casting and cuttlefish bone casting, selecting diamonds, gem-quality turquoise, or other precious stones for the elegant jewelry he creates.

One of Golsh's contemporaries and Kenneth Begay's oldest child, Harvey (b. 1938), appeared to be following in his father's footsteps when he started working at the White Hogan while still in high school. But Harvey Begay had different plans for his future. He enrolled in Arizona State University

Ric Charlie at the Heard Museum Guild Indian Fair & Market, 2006.

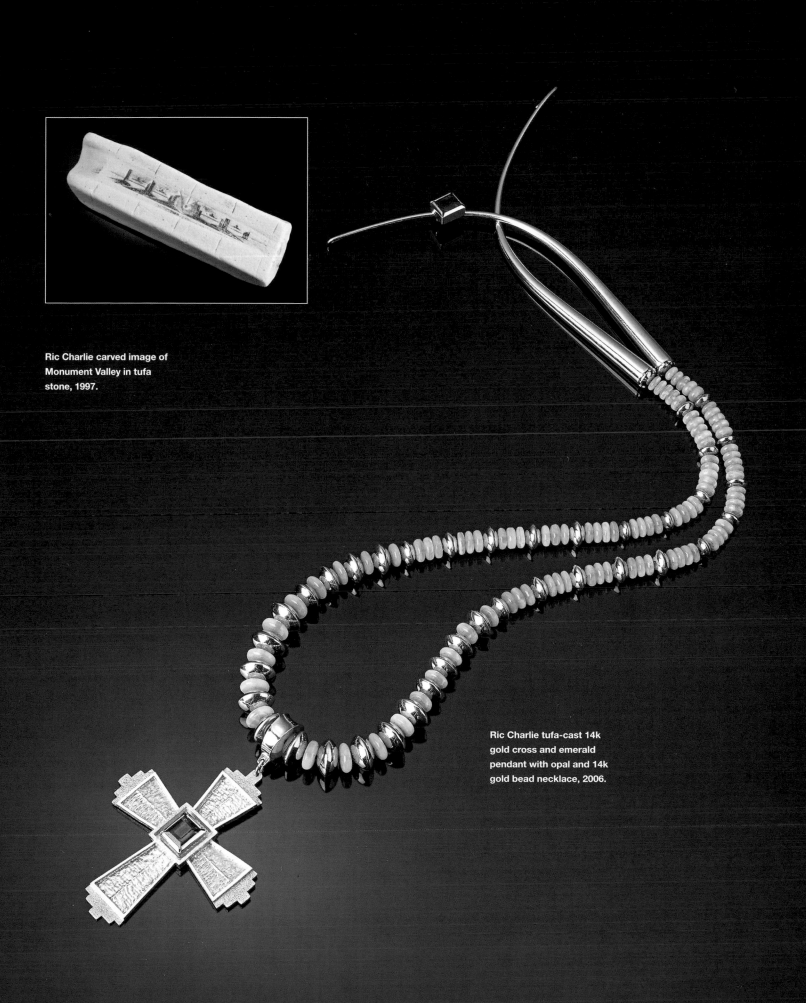

Ric Charlie carved image of
Monument Valley in tufa
stone, 1997.

Ric Charlie tufa-cast 14k
gold cross and emerald
pendant with opal and 14k
gold bead necklace, 2006.

and continued to work at the White Hogan, but graduated in 1961 with a bachelor of science degree in aeronautics. He joined the U.S. Navy and served one tour in the Vietnam War, where he flew in a fighter squadron. He left the military in 1965 and continued his interest in flying by working for McDonnell Douglas in St. Louis. During that employment he flight-tested F4 Phantom jets until 1970, at which point he began to devote himself to jewelry making.

Harvey Begay often refers to his Navajo heritage in the designs he creates. He combines traditional techniques and materials, but sometimes chooses gold, as in the 1997 tufa-cast 14k gold bracelet that has a more traditional coral for the setting. His designs also refer to inspirational American Indian lifeways or creative works, such as ancient pottery designs from Arizona. He often executes his creations in nontraditional techniques such as lost wax casting or uses nontraditional materials such as diamonds in his work.

Begay also learned the technique of diamond setting from French jeweler Pierre Touraine and worked alongside him beginning in 1979. Begay's works were featured in the 1974 and 1979 collector's issues of *Arizona Highways*. Although Begay

lives in Colorado, his jewelry has been featured in galleries in the Southwest since 1979.

Another jeweler who learned techniques from Pierre Touraine was Charles Supplee. Charles's brother, Don, is a self-taught jeweler who also works in tufa casting. Don Supplee (Hopi/French, b. 1965) began making jewelry around 1989. He learned the rudiments of jewelry techniques from his brother and experimented on his own to develop additional skills.

Navajo jeweler Ric Charlie (b. 1959) began experimenting with tufa casting while still a high school student in Tuba City, Arizona, in 1973. After he graduated, Charlie was awarded sports scholarships to Arizona State University and the University of Arizona in Tucson. This also gave him the opportunity to study jewelry making and design. Charlie admired the work of Preston Monongye and Charles Loloma and, in 1978, decided to teach himself tufa casting, a technique not taught in his formal university studies.

There are two ways that Charlie distinguishes his work. One is through the rich colors he accomplishes in his cast designs by adding liver of sulphur to the silver. Hues of gold, rust, purple, and blue give the jewelry a painted appearance. The other

Above, left: Ric Charlie tufa-cast 18k gold bracelet with a design of Monument Valley and Candelaria turquoise, 2006.

Above, right: Steve LaRance tufa-cast silver bracelet, 2006.

Opposite: Anthony Lovato tufa-cast silver pendant with onyx, 2006.

distinction is the incorporation of a tufa-cast design of Monument Valley. On a trip in the 1970s to visit his grandparents, Charlie became concerned that Monument Valley was inaccessible to Navajo people. He mainly uses imagery of this natural beauty on the interior of his bracelets and reverse sides of buckles, but occasionally on the visible side of bracelets.

In the mid-1990s, Charlie shared a studio with Marilyn Denipah (Ohkay-Owingeh/Navajo, b. 1959) and her husband Steve LaRance (Hopi, b. 1958). There, Charlie showed Denipah and LaRance tufa-casting techniques. LaRance had an interest in art at an early age and was encouraged by his Hopi uncles to study art. As a young boy growing up in Moencopi, he was involved with traditional arts and crafts, and he carved katsina dolls of cottonwood root. LaRance took a jewelry class while he was a student at Grey Hills High School in Tuba City, Arizona, in the mid-1970s. He and Denipah each studied at the Institute of American Indian Arts in Santa Fe, and Denipah later received a bachelor of arts degree from Northern Arizona University in Flagstaff.

Denipah was originally drawn to painting, while LaRance's work with stone carving led him to sculpture. Their interest in jewelry grew while sharing the studio with Ric Charlie, and the couple began making jewelry using tufa casting. Even though Charles Loloma worked mainly with tufa casting and the complex inlay of stones, it is unusual for a Hopi jeweler working today to choose tufa casting rather than the overlay technique. LaRance indicates that this was a conscious effort. As a Hopi artist, he has looked for a different niche in American Indian art to explore. Making the transition from direct stone sculpture to carving into tufa was not too difficult for LaRance. Both techniques involve carving, of course, but with tufa carving one carves into the stone. As LaRance notes, "Tufa carving is more delicate, and it involves carving by reverse order. After casting, when you pull out the work in metal, you see the results."[8]

LaRance leaves areas of the silver rough after casting and polishes other areas. He also draws images from nature and from petroglyphs. He signs his work with his Hopi name, "Wikviya," usually by carving it into the tufa stone and casting, which creates the name in relief.

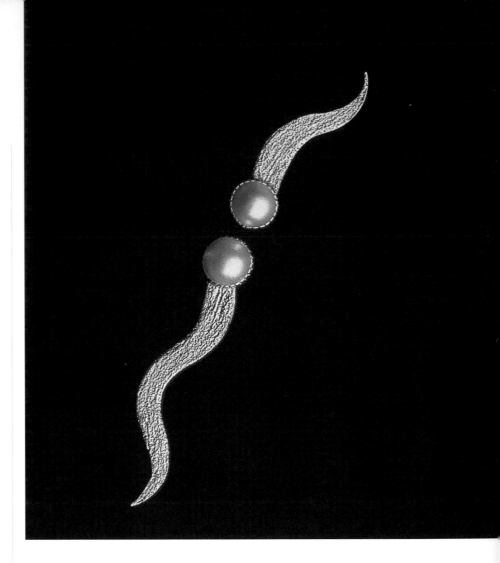

Yazzie Johnson and Gail Bird 18k gold tufa-cast earrings with mabe pearls, 2000.

Another artist who excels in casting is Santo Domingo jeweler Anthony Lovato (b. 1958). Lovato grew up in a family of jewelers that included his grandfather Santiago Leo Coriz, who taught Lovato casting techniques. In addition to his tufa-cast jewelry, Lovato is known for his large-scale canteens and vessels. His father, Sedelio F. Lovato, also made tufa-cast jewelry, and his mother, Mary Lovato, is an accomplished jeweler who is known for her shell pendants with inlaid stones.

Lovato helped his parents sell their jewelry under the portal in Santa Fe when he was just a boy. He graduated from the Institute of American Indian Arts in Santa Fe with an associate of arts degree in 1978. For the next two years, he worked at the Museum of Northern Arizona and took design classes at Northern Arizona University in Flagstaff and later at the University of Colorado in Boulder.[9]

Lovato often uses a corn image on his tufa-cast bracelets and on vessels. These large forms are cast in two parts on a sandstone slab and then soldered together using a welding torch. Lovato gets the rough sandstone from the Hopi reservation. Apart

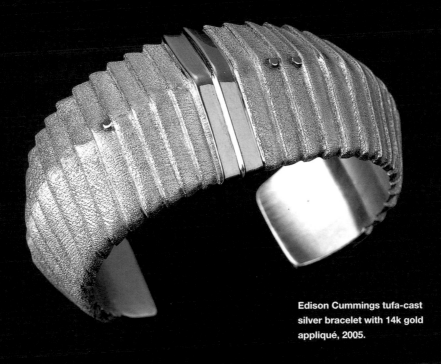

Edison Cummings tufa-cast
silver bracelet with 14k gold
appliqué, 2005.

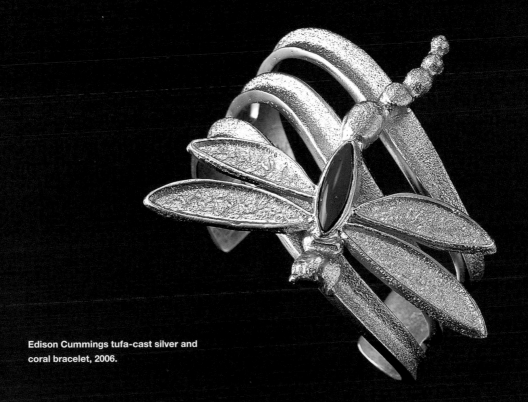

Edison Cummings tufa-cast silver and
coral bracelet, 2006.

James Little bracelet and
ring of cast 18k gold, opals,
diamonds, and coral, 2007.

from the large jars he makes, Lovato is best known for his tufa-cast, corn-maiden pendants, the concept of which was inspired by the work of Charles Loloma.

James Little (Navajo, b. 1947) is one of a few contemporary artists who works primarily using the lost wax–casting technique, a process where the artist creates a wax form that is replaced by molten metal. Little was encouraged by his brother to take art classes while a student at Rough Rock High School. Little learned to work with metal by studying at Navajo Community College in Many Farms, Arizona, with Kenneth Begay and by experimenting on his own.

In 1976, Little won top awards at the Heard Museum Guild Arts and Crafts Exhibit and at the Museum of Northern Arizona in Flagstaff. He was encouraged by a renowned photographer working for *Arizona Highways* magazine, Jerry Jacka, to show his work to gallerist Lovena Ohl. In 1981, Little was the third recipient of the Lovena Ohl Foundation Award, a fund established to help young artists. He also received the award in 1982 and 1983. He was among a small group of artists who worked in a contemporary style and in gold rather than silver. Little has continued to explore creatively and to use gold and diamonds in his work.

Fabrication

Fabrication is a technique of creating jewelry or metalwork by shaping the metal and embellishing it through a variety of means. One technique known as raising is a process of taking a flat sheet of metal, often silver but at times copper or brass, and hammering it into a form. Fabrication might include additional embellishments such as forcing a design into the surface through repoussé decoration or stamping or piercing the metal to form a design. Other design elements might be added through appliqué, a process of using heat to fuse a decorative metal element onto a metal surface.

Fabrication is one of the earliest techniques or combination of techniques used to create jewelry. Early silversmiths made their own sheets of silver by melting U.S. or Mexican coins to form an ingot and then hammering it into a shape. They also added designs to the surface with an awl. In this process, also called rocker engraving, patterns are impressed into the surface of the metal to create a design.

Early silversmiths were ingenious in their creation of diverse forms. Small tobacco canteens were some of the earliest containers made in the late 1800s, but hinged lidded boxes were also made after 1900. These were often embellished with designs or with the addition of turquoise, or, at times and depending upon the maker, more complex inlays of turquoise, coral, shell, or jet were added.

Key to any contemporary creation is the shape or form. Beginning in the 1950s, the silversmiths who worked at the White Hogan with John Bonnell—Kenneth Begay, Johnnie Mike Begay, Allan, Ivan, and George Kee—set new standards for unusually shaped metal containers, often combining them with ironwood. In 1990, Edison Cummings (b. 1962), a young Navajo jeweler who learned the basics of silversmithing from classes at the Institute of American Indian Arts in Santa Fe and later at Arizona State University in Tempe, began working at the White Hogan in Scottsdale. Cummings worked with the original owner's son, Jon Bonnell, to develop shapes and designs. Cummings followed the tradition established by the Begays and Kees in conjunction with the White Hogan. In 1996, Cummings created a silver teapot with stamped designs and containing

Morris Robinson (Hopi, 1900–87) fabricated silver footed bowl with stamped rain cloud designs, 1950s.

Edison Cummings fabricated silver teapot with iron-wood, 1996.

Cheyenne Harris silver, nickel silver, 14k gold, and white gold flatware set, 1997.

Edison Cummings silver and stainless flatware, 1997.

an ironwood handle and tip of the lid for the Heard Museum Guild Indian Fair & Market.

Cummings calls the process of shaping the metal into these complex forms "stretching the metal."[10] The emphasis is on the elegant shape, which is accented only minimally by stamp work. The shape of the ironwood handle is compatible with the shape of the teapot and further enhances the overall appearance of the item. At the 2006 Indian Market in Santa Fe, Cummings won the Best of Classification award for jewelry for another silver teapot with ironwood used for the handle and tip of the lid. When opened, the tip of the lid rests perfectly on the top of the handle.

Cummings also accomplished another White

Cheyenne Harris silver, 24k gold, and nickel pins, 1990–93. One pin has an accent of lapis lazuli.

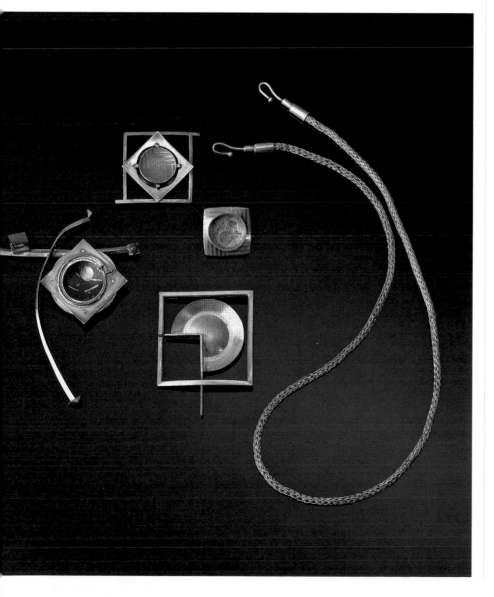

Cheyenne Harris silver, 24k gold, and nickel pins, 1997 and 1998.

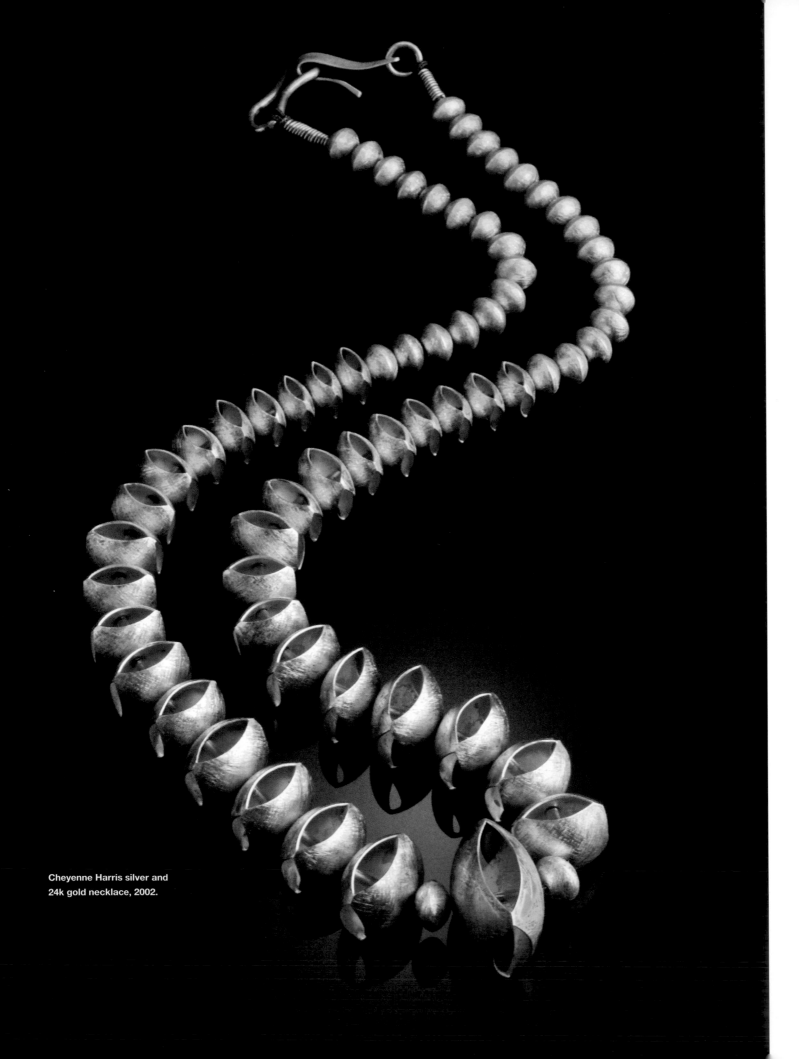

Cheyenne Harris silver and
24k gold necklace, 2002.

Near right: Monica King "Under False Pretense," silver, mild steel, nickel, and jet ring, 1998.

Far right: Myron Panteah silver pin with designs in pierce work and 14k gold and silver appliqué. The stone is a Bruneau jasper, 2004.

Myron Panteah "Impressed Clown," silver with pierce work and 14k gold appliqué, 2002.

Below: Kee Yazzie, Jr., silver bracelet and earrings with designs in pierce work and 14k gold appliqué, 2002.

Right: Kee Yazzie, Jr., silver seed jar with pierce work designs representing the stars and sun, 1990s.

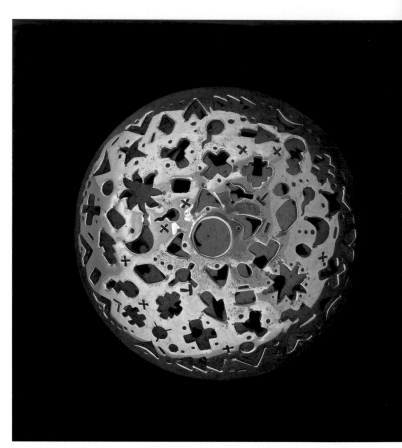

Right: Christina Eustace fabricated silver floral design pin with silver drop appliqué, 1983.

Left: Christina Eustace at the Heard Museum Guild Indian Fair & Market, 2006.

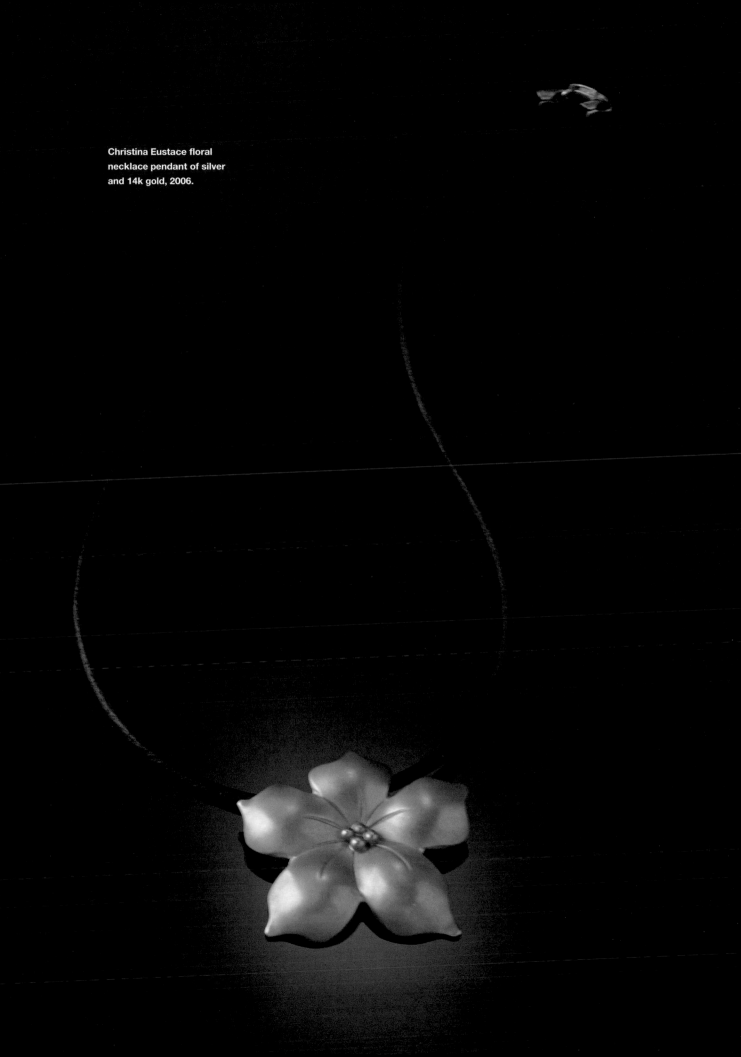

Christina Eustace floral
necklace pendant of silver
and 14k gold, 2006.

Hogan tradition of designing and fabricating table service ware or flatware. For a set made in 1997, he formed the handles out of silver, and added prefabricated stainless steel blades and tines.

Within the same year, he had begun to make all components of the flatware, including the blades and tines, out of silver. Cummings has continued to explore the complexities of service ware, occasionally making teapots and flatware in addition to a diverse array of bracelets, earrings, and pendant necklaces he has made through the years.

Another artist who has created elegant contemporary flatware and is also a university-trained jeweler is Cheyenne Harris (Navajo/Northern Cheyenne, b. 1963). Harris began formal studies of metalwork at universities in Arizona and earned her bachelor of fine arts degree from Arizona State University (ASU) in 1985. Harris continued to refine her metalworking skills by taking graduate-level classes from ASU and from the University of Massachusetts in North Dartmouth. Harris is a fourth-generation jeweler who learned silversmithing techniques from her mother, Roberta Multine Tso, who had studied silversmithing with Kenneth Begay at Navajo Community College in Many Farms, Arizona. As a young girl, Harris remembers watching her mother create jewelry on the family's kitchen table, which had been temporarily converted into a workbench. By the age of five, Harris was helping her mother with some preliminary tasks. Harris credits Begay's influence on her own work through her mother's education-

Navaasya fabricated silver chain bracelet, 2002.

al experiences and the inclusion of his work in her personal jewelry collection.

Harris likes to meld metals and contemporary designs. In 1997, she made a flatware set, but she incorporated sterling silver, nickel silver, 14k gold, and white gold, all delicately noted in her tiny script along with her name and the date on the individual pieces of the set.

Harris also accomplishes elegant shapes in silver and enhances them with light accents of yellow gold. Although she is best known for her bracelets and necklaces, she has on occasion made intricate pins with compelling shapes that incorporate those same light touches of gold in delicate designs.

Monica King (Pima/Navajo/Tohono O'odham, b. 1957) is the first American Indian artist to complete a master of fine arts degree with an emphasis on jewelry from Arizona State University. What makes King's jewelry uniquely different are not only the concepts and designs, but also the interactive qualities of the works. In 1998, while completing the project for her master of arts degree, King developed several conceptual works. One of those, a ring titled "Under False Pretense," is about corporate drilling of natural resources on American Indian lands. At a glance, the ring, with its movable parts, appears different and intriguing. When examined with the title, it is apparent that the movable part is a drill and the drill bit is local jet. King is making a statement about her objection to the destruction of the land that occurs in the process of removing coal or uranium from Native lands. Also, one side of the ring has a stylized face of an Indian person depicted in a stepped motif while the opposite has a stylized motif of an American Indian home. The placement of the drill between the Indian face and the depiction of the home symbolically represents industry cutting through the community. King not only used silver and brass in the fabrication of the ring, but also mild steel, another symbolic representation of industry.

King first learned about jewelry making as a sophomore in high school in Coolidge, Arizona. In 1975, she moved to Santa Fe to begin her junior year of high school at the Institute of American Indian Arts (IAIA) where she studied jewelry-making techniques with Navajo silversmith Jimmy Yazzie. She continued at IAIA to complete an associate of

arts degree and studied with Millard Holbrook, who taught her different fabrication techniques. King went on to study at the Philadelphia College of Art (now the University of the Arts), where she received a bachelor of fine arts degree in 1979.

King has developed a distinctive style and has explored the use of nontraditional materials such as steel. Because she likes the interactive nature of jewelry, she at times uses rivets or creates small cogs to make things move or spin. Her work not only has an aesthetic appeal but is also conceptually intriguing.

Two jewelers, Myron Panteah and Kee Yazzie, Jr., are known for their designs that are accomplished by piercing the metal. Panteah (Navajo/Zuni, b. 1966) would observe his father, Martin, who made channelwork jewelry and his grandmother, Sybil, who made needlepoint jewelry, and he would play with his father's jewelry tools. Panteah experimented with jewelry making as a boy and became more interested during high school in Tohatchi, New Mexico, when he took jewelry classes. Initially, he tried a variety of techniques, including stamp work, for which he made his own stamps. While still in high school, he also worked in overlay and inlay and tried different techniques and designs that he saw in *Arizona Highways* magazine.

In 1995, after an injury to his right hand, Panteah switched from inlay work, which requires thumb and first digit dexterity, to a different style using fabrication techniques. He received a fellowship award from the Southwestern Association of American Indian Arts (SWAIA) in 1998 and used the funds to take workshops at Duane Maktima's Pueblo Five Institute. There he learned texturing and forging and became exposed to a range of contemporary work through the jewelers who taught classes.[11] He distinguishes his jewelry not only by the pierce work designs but also by texturing the metal through the use of steel wool in a rolling mill.

Kee Yazzie, Jr. (Navajo, b. 1969) is a self-taught artist who began making jewelry in 1995. He grew up in Provo, Utah, and attended Utah Valley Community College, where he studied architectural and drafting design. He learned jewelry-making techniques by trial and error and experimentation, teaching himself some basics such as soldering and working with gold. Navajo jeweler Ray Scott showed Yazzie some finishing-work

Linda Lou Metoxen miniature silver jar with lid, 2006.

Fritz Casuse ring of silver, 14k gold, and gemstone, 2007. One ring fits inside the other, allowing the ring to be worn two different ways.

techniques. He also took two workshops at Duane Maktima's Pueblo Five Design Institute in 1998. Yazzie admired the silver seed jars that Norbert Peshlakai made and the textures he accomplished and began to hammer-texture his own work. To acquire a textured surface, Yazzie takes a nail and strikes it repeatedly over the silver. Some of his designs are inspired by petroglyphs from Jeddito near Keams Canyon, Arizona.

Hopi jeweler Phil Navaasya's jewelry of hand-fabricated, multiple-link chains is distinctive. Born at the Hopi village of Old Oraibi in 1944, Navaasya's career includes formal studies of art that resulted in a bachelor of arts degree from California State University in Fresno and a master of arts degree from the University of Montana in Missoula.

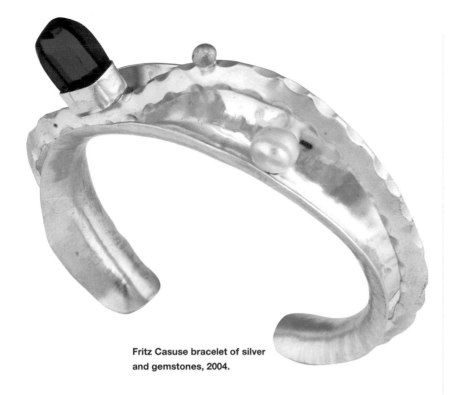

Fritz Casuse bracelet of silver and gemstones, 2004.

Navaasya holds the honor of being the first artist to receive the Best of Show Award at the Indian Market in Santa Fe in 1977, when the award was first established. His jewelry has been shown worldwide since his first exhibit at the Heard Museum in 1973.

Christina Alice Eustace (Zuni/Cochiti, b. 1954) was the seventh of thirteen children born to Felicita and Benjamin Eustace. Christina Eustace grew up in Albuquerque, New Mexico, and her family spent time both at Zuni with her father's family and at Cochiti with her mother's. As a child, she watched her mother, Felicita, make traditional Zuni-style cluster work and inlay jewelry and saw her father carve stone leaf shapes and fabricate silver leaf designs. Eustace's mother learned jewelry-making techniques, including petit point, from her Zuni sisters-in-law. She either helped her husband make jewelry or created her traditional Zuni-style work. Benjamin Eustace developed a carved leaf design that Christina Eustace emulated at the age of thirteen when she began making jewelry. She carved turquoise and coral leaf forms in

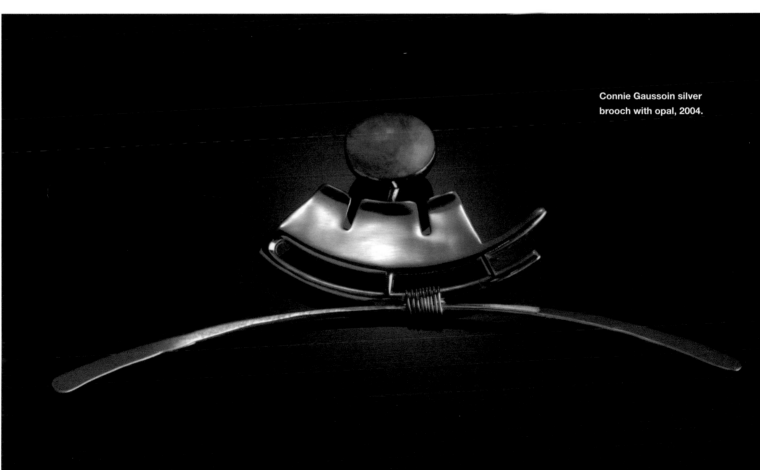

Connie Gaussoin silver brooch with opal, 2004.

her father's style and initially made them into tie tacks. As she developed her skills, she made more elaborate pieces.

Eustace graduated from high school at age seventeen and continued to work in her father's style into her late teens. At age nineteen or twenty, she began to do stained glass and developed her ideas for one of her signature designs, a floral pattern. She pursued a bachelor of fine arts degree at the University of New Mexico in Albuquerque, full-time for four years and then continued her studies part time. At the end of her studies at UNM, she began to take jewelry classes, where she learned several processes, including repoussé and lost wax casting. She used the repoussé technique to develop a floral pattern in silver, and she continues to make floral patterns today.

In 1985, she moved to New York to challenge herself and experience a creative change in her work. She continued to sell jewelry at Dewey Gallery in Santa Fe and Gallery 10 in Scottsdale; she also sold her work in Manhattan. She did lapidary work in New York, and after living and working there for five years, she returned to New Mexico. Eustace now focuses on silver and gold jewelry creations that emphasize form and texture as well as lapidary work.

Linda Lou Metoxen (Navajo, b. 1964) is a metalsmith artist who makes raised and fabricated containers, bowls, and goblets. When she was attending Shiprock High School, Metoxen and five other students were mentored by sculptor Oreland Joe.[12] After graduation, Metoxen attended Dine College in Shiprock and then the Institute of American Indian Arts in Santa Fe. She continued her studies at the University of Wisconsin in Madison where she received a bachelor of fine arts degree and then a master of fine arts degree in 1996. Initially, she made large stone sculptures, but she later developed an interest in making jewelry. In 2006, she created her first miniature silver pot with a female figure on the lid. Like her larger works, the miniature was formed from one sheet of silver.

Fritz Casuse (Navajo, b. 1968) started making jewelry around 2000. He took drawing and ceramics classes at Tohatchi High School and also studied sculpture at the Institute of American Indian Arts. Although some of his relatives made jewelry, he never approached them for help. Instead, Casuse learned some preliminary jewelry techniques at IAIA from instructor Lane Coulter. After he graduated in 1996, his aunt bought him some silversmithing tools. In 1999 at the Poeh Arts Center, Casuse took sculpture classes from Nelson Tsosie and also took tufa-casting classes from Joel McHorse. In 2000, Casuse entered his first art fair at the Eight Northern Pueblos. Recently, Casuse has taught classes at the Poeh Center and found that teaching jewelry techniques has strengthened his skills as a jeweler. Much of his work retains sculptural elements.

Connie Tsosie Gaussoin (Navajo/Picuris, b. 1948) makes traditional and contemporary sterling silver and gold jewelry. While a teenager, Gaussoin sang for four and a half years with the group Up With People, traveling through Western Canada, Central America, and Scandinavian countries. She later attended Navajo Community College in Many Farms, Arizona, and the Institute of American Indian Arts in Santa Fe. She views her professional silversmithing career as officially beginning when she entered jewelry in the Indian Market in Santa Fe in 1971. Gaussoin has two sons, David and Wayne, who are active jewelers featured in chapter four. She has served as a silversmith instructor for Eight Northern Indian Pueblos Council, and she and David conducted a tufa-casting workshop at the Heard Museum in 2003.

Navajo silver squash blossom earrings, early 1900s. The blossoms were formed by doming.

Navajo silver concho belt, c. 1900.

Doming

Silver concho belts and beads are both shaped by a technique called *doming*. The dome shape is the historic shape of the conchos, which were first made in the Southwest as early as 1880.[13] The earliest conchos were round with a diamond slot in the center. Later, when metal loops were added to the reverse sides, silversmiths emulated the diamond slots by creating the pattern in the centers of conchos.

To make a domed shape, a section of silver is placed over a concave form, usually a depression in a stump of wood, and hit with a hammer until the silver conforms to the shape of the depression. Today, a silversmith might begin a concho by cutting a sheet of silver into a round or oval shape before doming. Others might work in an older style, melting silver and then forming an ingot by pouring the molten metal into a mold. Once the metal has cooled and formed the ingot, it is hammered into the desired shape.

Beads are formed by soldering together two silver pieces that have been shaped into domes. Most silversmiths will polish the joint to create a smooth bead. Historically, some buttons and bead halves were made by hammering coins directly and, in some instances, the image and wording of the coin is still visible.

Silversmith Perry Shorty (Navajo, b. 1964) makes silver jewelry in the traditional way by melting silver into ingots and hammering them into shapes to form conchos for belts and beads for necklaces. A first-generation silversmith, Shorty became interested in jewelry making while working in a silver supply store in Gallup, New Mexico.[14] He worked as an apprentice with his brother-in-law, Ernie Lister, from 1986 to 1990. He won his first major award for cluster jewelry in 1994 at the Gallup Inter-Tribal Ceremonial, and he was awarded a Southwestern Association of Indian Arts (SWAIA) fellowship in 1995.

Mike Bird-Romero (San Juan, b. 1946) is known for his silver bead and cross necklaces. Beginning in 1990, Bird-Romero and his wife, Allison, researched historic cross necklaces. Allison wrote a book about the necklaces called *Heart of the Dragonfly*, which was published in 1992. Mike

Perry Shorty silver concho
belt formed from ingots,
2006.

Perry Shorty demonstrates
silversmithing techniques in
June 2006 at a seminar organized by Martha Struever.

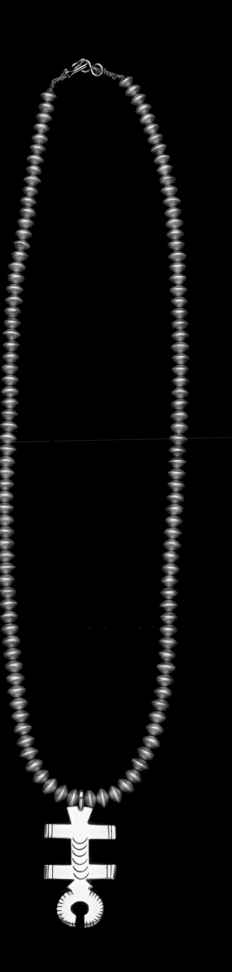

Left: Mike Bird-Romero silver bead and cross necklace, 1991.

Below: Debbie Silversmith silver beads, 2005.

Bird-Romero created more than 140 cross pendants inspired by the historic Pueblo and Navajo jewelry he and Allison saw in museum collections, private collections, and historic photographs.

Bird-Romero grew up in a household that encouraged art. His mother, Lorencita Bird, was an accomplished weaver and educator, and his sister Evelyn Quintana is an accomplished weaver as well. Bird-Romero learned some basic metalsmithing skills while in junior high school. As a young boy, he also observed jewelers Julian Lovato, Mark Chee, and Antonio Duran when the three men lived and worked at San Juan. Apart from those experiences, Bird-Romero is largely self-taught, deriving what information he could by

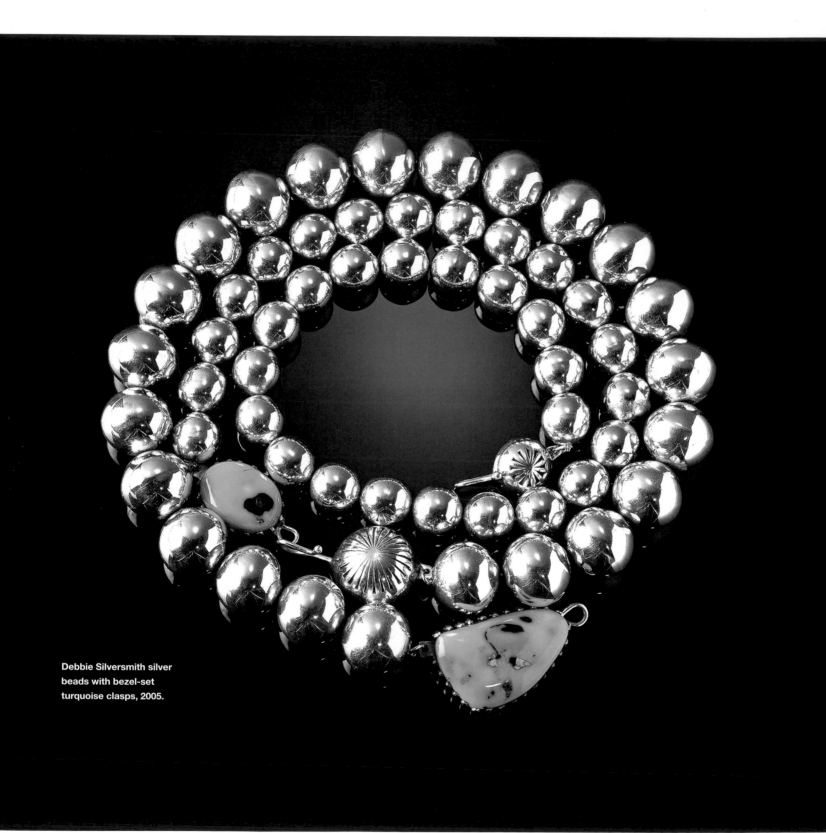

**Debbie Silversmith silver
beads with bezel-set
turquoise clasps, 2005.**

Jennifer Curtis reversible concho belt of silver and turquoise with stamp work, 2006.

Jennifer Curtis reverse side of concho belt, 2006.

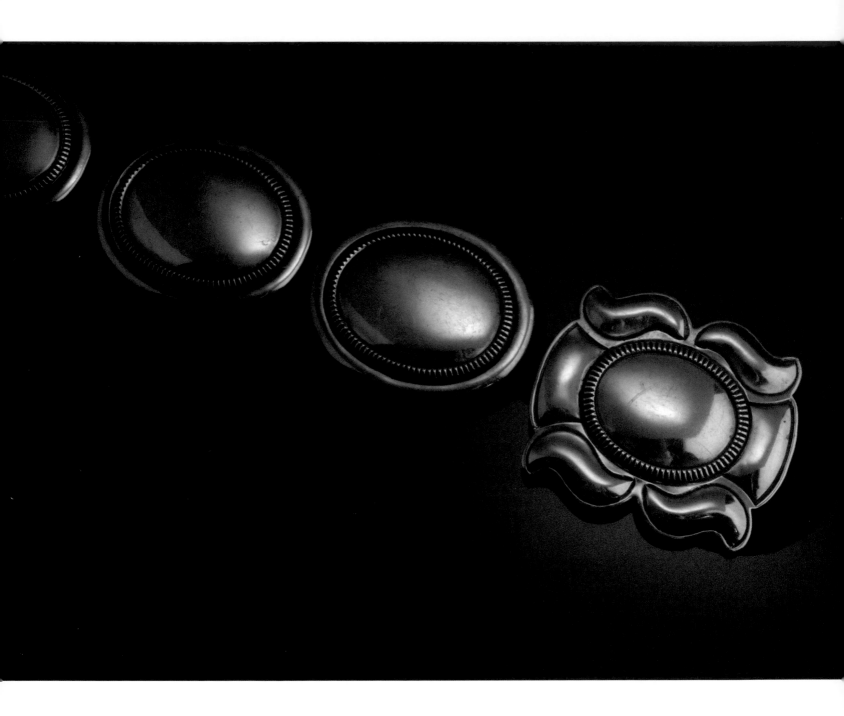

Cippy Crazy Horse silver
belt with domed conchos
and repoussé on the buckle,
2000.

reading books and experimenting. He is known for his classic designed jewelry that combines silverwork with unusual stones.

Debbie Silversmith (Navajo, b. 1957) was instructed in jewelry-making techniques by her grandfather Kenneth Begay, and her designs are often inspired by his classical works. As a child, Silversmith watched her grandfather work. He taught her how to make jewelry "by hand, the old way."[15] The first type of jewelry Begay taught her to make was beads. Silversmith made her first saleable work by age eleven. When Silversmith was in high school, she worked side by side with her grandfather, who stressed perfection. Begay taught her the old techniques of tufa casting, using tufa he acquired near Steamboat Springs, Arizona, and coating it with juniper ash. At times, they employed another old-style technique and buffed the tufa-cast silver totally by hand.

Silversmith graduated from Chinle High School and attended Navajo Community College for one and a half years. She specializes in clean silver designs with defined lines and smooth silver beads. She uses her grandfather's tools and has been inspired by some of his designs, including the swirls he developed that represent water and life.

Jennifer Curtis (Navajo, b. 1964) learned about silversmithing from her father, Thomas Curtis, Sr., who works in a traditional style. As a child of about eight years old, she first became interested in her father's work when she played in his shop. Curtis's only training was with her father. She began to make silver jewelry on her own after graduating from high school in Holbrook, Arizona. Curtis began to work more seriously around 1987, and gradually developed her own designs, separating her work from her father's. Jennifer uses fabrication techniques in her jewelry creations. For some time, she had an idea for a belt that would be reversible. After gaining more experience, she determined how to execute the concept. In 2006, she completed the belt, creating one side with stamped designs only and the other with Morenci turquoise in addition to stamp work.

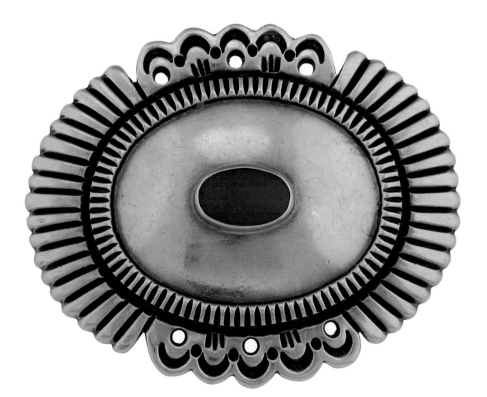

Cippy Crazy Horse domed silver buckle with coral, 1996.

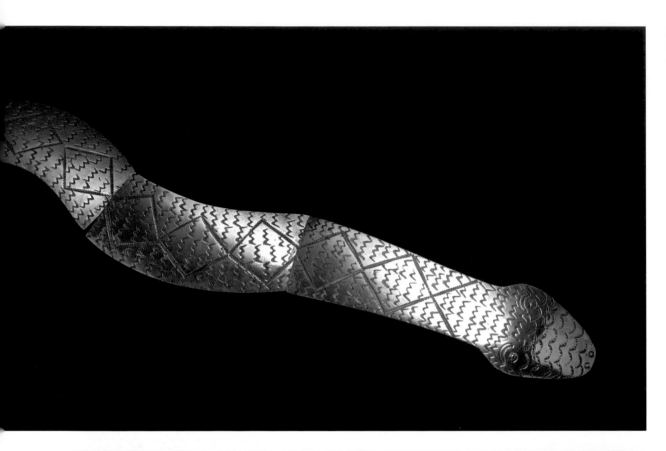

Navajo stamp-work silver belt in the shape of a rattlesnake, c. 1940.

Norbert Peshlakai silver seed jar with several of his characteristic stamped designs, including a rabbit, horse, butterfly, and Cowboy Slim, 2001.

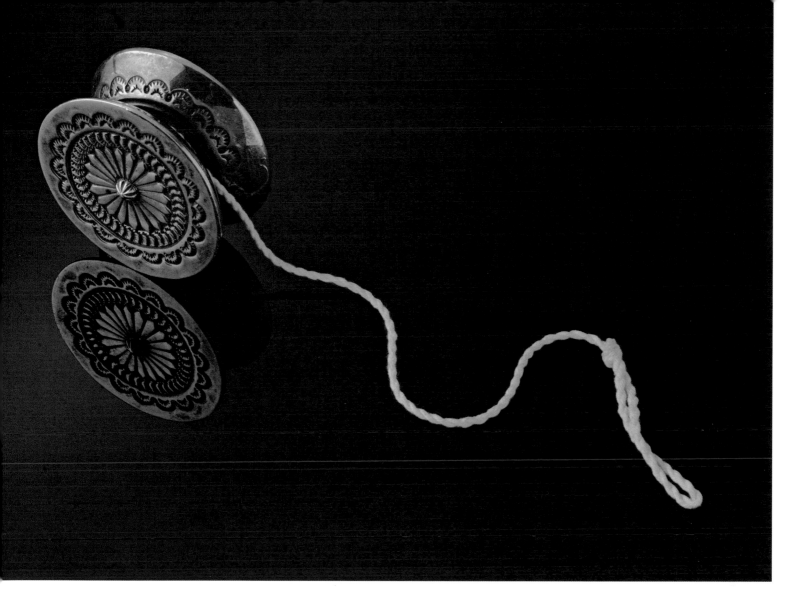

Stamp Work

Stamping is a method of impressing a design in silver by placing a stamp or die on the silver and striking the other end of the die with a hammer to create the design. It is one of the more frequently used techniques of decorating silver jewelry.

In the 1880s and 1890s, traders in Arizona and New Mexico imported tools for Navajo silversmiths that included fine files that could be made into stamps. Stamp work became a frequently employed decorative technique with the introduction of fine files, and silversmiths were making their own stamps by the late 1880s.[16] Silversmiths made stamps not only from files but also from other metal forms, including railroad spikes, car pistons, nails, bolts, chisels, rivets, and other useful metal shapes.

Stamping offered a method of accomplishing deep and complex curvilinear patterns to silver jewelry and changed the decorative elements dramatically. Once a die was made or acquired, stamping was a quicker, bolder, and potentially fuller way to create a design. Prior to the use of stamps, a band bracelet might have been enhanced with a chisel to round the edges or create pointed ridges on the band, and simple geometric designs were also filed into silver surfaces.[17]

Although curved patterns had been possible with rocker engraving—the technique of using an awl to scratch or impress a design into silver—the artist often made the design only faintly impressed in the surface or, at times, made the impression deeper, though finely made. Rocker engraving was quickly replaced by stamp work among southwestern jewelers—although some items continued to be decorated by this method. One belt in the Heard Museum Collection thoroughly decorated with stamp work is in the shape of a rattlesnake. It is made in sections to replicate the curve of a crawling snake, and the rattler is turned at the end to form the belt latch. The Heard Museum founder, Maie Bartlett Heard, purchased this unusual belt from Mike Kirk around 1940. It was made by a silversmith in Manuelito, New Mexico.

Stamping has been used continually throughout the last century. Though design concepts have changed, it remains one of the primary techniques employed to decorate jewelry. Today, many jewelers use older dies, make their own dies, or use a combination of the two. Some jewelers make two or more dies to create one pattern. Stamping can be combined with other techniques, such as repoussé or appliqué, in jewelry fabrication.

One jeweler known for his elaborate and complex stamp work is Norbert Peshlakai (Navajo, b. 1953). A fourth generation silversmith, Peshlakai took art classes in high school. By the time he was in college at Haskell Junior College in Kansas, he was interested in painting and made plans to enroll in a class. When he discovered that the class was about house painting rather than easel painting, he switched to a jewelry class instead. He studied at Haskell for about three and a half years and then returned to Crystal, New Mexico, where he continued to make jewelry.

Peshlakai is best known for his fine stamp work and the miniature seed jars he creates. Making them led him to develop miniature dies to create the small decorative patterns on the jars. He has customized basic tools into specialized instruments, and made masonry nails into small dies, often using several dies to form a single motif. His Mimbres-style rabbit design incorporates ten or more dies to form the whiskers, eyes, legs, and other body parts.

Peshlakai's creativity is not limited to the stamp work designs. In 1999, he created a stamped silver tie, formed in sections to resemble a man's tie. Peshlakai's sense of humor is revealed in the stamp work, such as his hallmark cowboy design he has named Cowboy Slim. Norbert recalls, "In 1998, I decided to do a necktie out of sterling silver, since I saw a student in my basic jewelry class when I taught several years earlier at Western New Mexico University who wore a commercial necktie made out of stainless steel with jump rings and a hook chain neck piece. I purchased an 18-gauge sterling scrap sheet, and I held it against my chest and told my wife, Linda, 'I am going to make a necktie out of the silver sheet' but did not tell her how I was going to make it." According to Pesh-

Norbert Peshlakai stamp-work silver tie, 1999. Cowboy Slim is in the top segment of the tie.

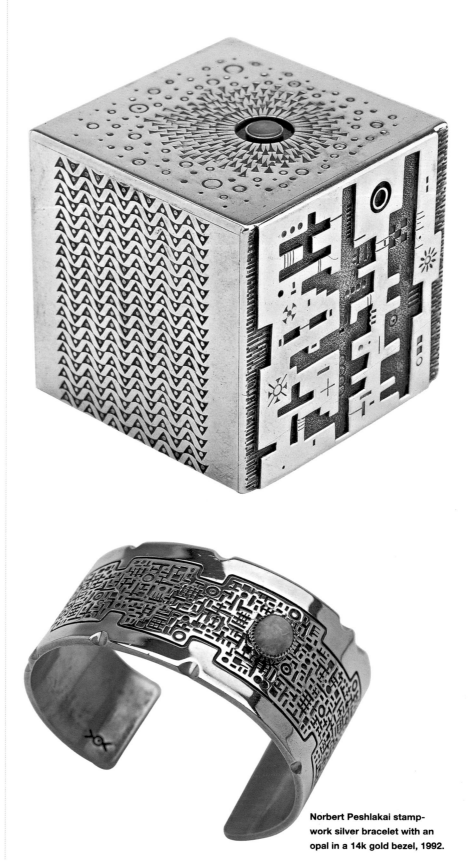

Norbert Peshlakai, "The Cube," a silver paper-weight, 1996. Peshlakai used different techniques to make different designs on each side.

lakai's wife, Linda, "When Norbert told me he was going to make a necktie with the silver sheet, I asked him, 'Wouldn't that poke the person wearing the tie?' Little did I know the tie would be designed into small pieces attached with small hand-made chain. It came out beautiful when it was completed."[18]

Peshlakai has placed Cowboy Slim on other creative works including one of his silver seed jars. Cowboy Slim is formed with seven different stamps. Each boot is a separate stamp. The other designs on the jar represent nature and are also formed by multiple stamps—eight stamps are used for the horse, three for the butterfly, and five each for the turtle and small rabbit. The surface is punch-textured with a punch hammer. At times, Peshlakai does the stamp work first and then hammers the texture. At other times, he reverses this process.

Although he is known for stamp work, Peshlakai's silversmithing skills are much broader. His ability to fashion the small, perfectly shaped miniature seed jars is uniquely his own. According to Peshlakai, "I learned basic traditional techniques and wanted to do something different, so I made bowls into different shapes and forms. Later, I went back into jewelry and started experimenting with various methods, using sandpaper, emery paper, and steel wool for texture. I would also hit it on rocks, do hammer texturing, and use needle files to do texturing. I like it because of the color—some of it is shiny and some is dull. When you heat up the silver it does get a thin layer of oxidation, and you can grind that off with emery paper. A lot of the time, I just leave the fire scale on. I just work around it."[19]

Peshlakai created an unusual form in 1996 when he made a sterling cube paperweight. The two-by-two-inch square cube was created with a different technique on each side. For one side, he

Norbert Peshlakai stamp-work silver bracelet with an opal in a 14k gold bezel, 1992.

Top: Norbert Peshlakai at the 48th Annual Heard Museum Guild Indian Fair & Market, 2006.

Above: Norbert Peshlakai's stamps, 2006.

stamped a sunshine design radiating from a single coral inset in the silver. For a second, he used appliqué and stamp work. For a third, he made a stamp-work wave design. For a fourth, he created a bird design in silver overlay. For a fifth, he used a number-22-gauge steel guitar string and hammered it onto the silver to make the impressed design. For the sixth, he used nine intricate stamps to make the design. The paperweight received a second prize at the Inter-Tribal Indian Ceremonial in Gallup in 1996. Peshlakai has stated that "The Cube" is a "bend-the-rule-type" piece that collectors or friends sometimes ask him to make.

Peshlakai began to use guitar wire for stamped designs quite by accident. After Haskell, he was experimenting with textures, and he tried hammering commercial wire he had placed on silver. This was only marginally successful, as the wire was not strong enough to withstand the hammering. Peshlakai often played guitar when he took breaks from his silversmithing. One day when a string broke, he got the idea to use the guitar wire in place of the commercial wire. He placed the guitar wire in the desired shape on a silver sheet, taped it, and then hammered to create the design.

Peshlakai combines stamp work designs with surface textures. Some of these are achieved by using different types of hammers. He used a ball peen hammer with a bezel file to texture the wings of a butterfly pin that is further embellished with stamp work and appliqué.

Sanford Storer (Navajo, b. 1961) also makes large stamp-work containers with fitted lids. Storer graduated from Gallup High School in 1979. He learned some silverworking techniques through informal studies with Stanley Parker and John Foutz in 1992 and 1993. Storer begins by drawing a design on paper and then precisely measuring it in silver. He cuts out the silver shape and then stamps the designs he has chosen for the piece. Next, he forms the work, cutting when necessary and soldering pieces together. The final touches on his highly polished silver objects may take hours.

Daniel "Sunshine" Reeves (Navajo, b. 1964) is known for his intricate stamp work and unusual creations. Reeves graduated from Tohatchi High School in 1983, and like his brother, Gary, he learned silverwork techniques from two of his brothers. Reeves has distinguished his work by the complex stamp work as well as the unusual forms such as tea sets, yoyos, picture frames, and even a train set. Reeves received recognition in 1997 when his eight-piece silver coffee set won Best of Show at Indian Market in Santa Fe, where over

Norbert Peshlakai silver stamp-work pin with hammer texture, appliqué, and Brazilian agate, 2001.

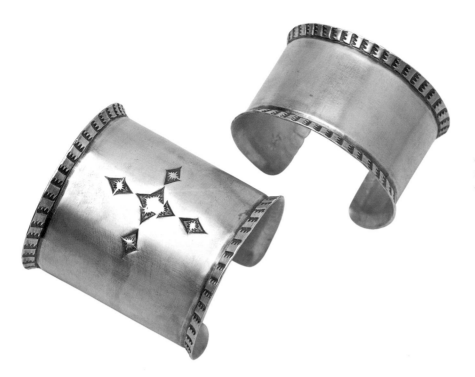

James Faks silver bracelets with stamp work, 2004.

James Faks silver buckle with stamp work, 2005.

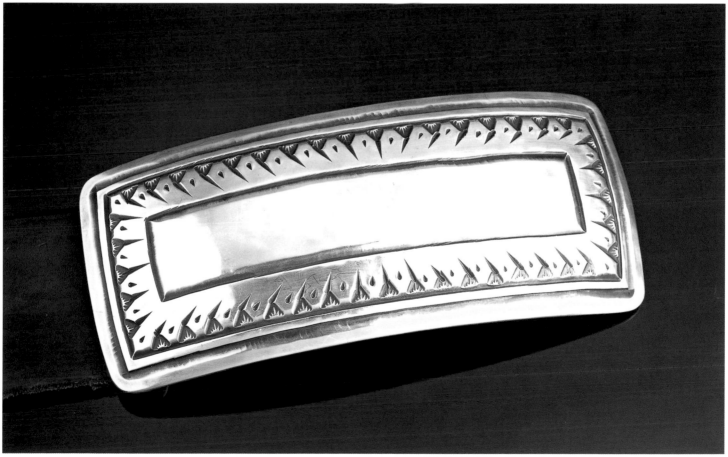

James Faks silver concho belt with stamp work, 2002.

Gibson Nez chisel-work silver bracelets with lapis lazuli and charoite, 2002.

1500 entries were submitted for judging. The following year at the same event, he won Best of Classification in Jewelry. Reeves also creates concho belts and squash blossom necklaces in addition to the unusual forms he makes.

Gibson Nez (Jicarilla Apache/Navajo, b. 1944) is a self-taught jeweler who often uses heavy-gauge silver or gold. Initially, he made rodeo chaps and other leatherwork with stamped designs, a technique he learned as a boy in the 4H club. Because of his leather-working skills, applying the stamping technique to silver came naturally to Nez. He began working with silver when he was twenty-four or twenty-five years old and continued to be involved in rodeo for thirty-five years. Nez is known for his fine chisel work accented by select stones.

Jake Livingston (Navajo/Zuni, b. 1945) is also a self-taught jeweler. Livingston learned jewelry-

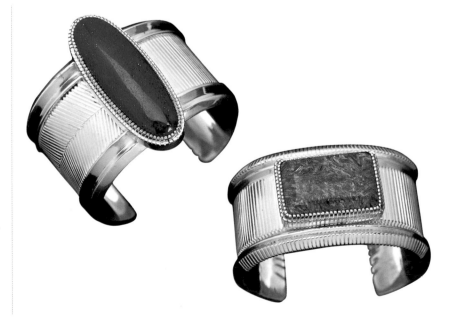

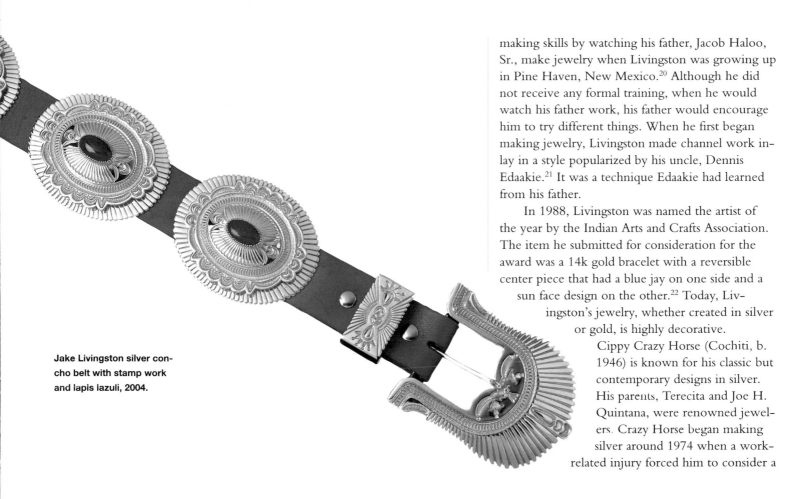

Jake Livingston silver concho belt with stamp work and lapis lazuli, 2004.

making skills by watching his father, Jacob Haloo, Sr., make jewelry when Livingston was growing up in Pine Haven, New Mexico.[20] Although he did not receive any formal training, when he would watch his father work, his father would encourage him to try different things. When he first began making jewelry, Livingston made channel work inlay in a style popularized by his uncle, Dennis Edaakie.[21] It was a technique Edaakie had learned from his father.

In 1988, Livingston was named the artist of the year by the Indian Arts and Crafts Association. The item he submitted for consideration for the award was a 14k gold bracelet with a reversible center piece that had a blue jay on one side and a sun face design on the other.[22] Today, Livingston's jewelry, whether created in silver or gold, is highly decorative.

Cippy Crazy Horse (Cochiti, b. 1946) is known for his classic but contemporary designs in silver. His parents, Terecita and Joe H. Quintana, were renowned jewelers. Crazy Horse began making silver around 1974 when a work-related injury forced him to consider a

Mike Bird-Romero silver pins with stamp work and turquoise, 2004.

different line of work. Prior to that, he attended Eastern New Mexico University in Portales,
had received an honorable discharge in 1972 after
joining the U.S. Navy, and had begun to work as
an electrician's assistant. When he started making
jewelry, he received encouragement from his wife,
Susan, and his father. He began by making silver
chains and gradually taught himself the old style of
silversmithing.

Crazy Horse developed a signature bracelet
with stamp-work lines after seeing a Michelin tire
track pattern in the mud when he helped someone
change a flat tire. The complex pattern is just one
of many designs Crazy Horse has created.

**Cippy Crazy Horse stamp-
work silver bracelet, 2001.**

**Sanford Storer stamp-work
silver container with lapis
lazuli, 2002.**

Repoussé

Repoussé is the metalsmithing technique of forming a design in relief by pressing the metal from the reverse side. The shapes are formed by the die that is placed on the reverse side of the metal and struck with a hammer. At times the silversmith will enhance the repoussé design by adding stamped designs on the front side of the metal around the edge of the repoussé design. Often, the metalsmith creates repoussé designs that are elliptically shaped. Historically, repoussé has been used to decorate bowguards, concho belts, and other silver objects of adornment. Often, the technique is applied to large format items such as horse headstalls, silver containers, or bracelets, but it can also be used to decorate smaller items such as a silver hairpin.

Navajo silver bowguard with repoussé, stamp work designs, and turquoise, early 1900s.

Navajo silver hairpin with repoussé and stamp work designs, early 1900s.

Contemporary artists have taken this technique and created new forms. For the 2006 Heard Museum Guild Indian Fair & Market, Edison Cummings created a silver purse with a floral-and-leaf design in repoussé that began near the purse clasp and extended over the back of the purse. The purse won the Best of Classification award for jewelry at the Heard Fair. Cummings utilizes repoussé to create bold forms on silver bracelets as well as to emphasize the properties of the silver through the technique.

In 2006, Cummings was commissioned by the Heard to make a silverwork item for the collection. The museum had been given five turquoise stones by a collector. Cummings was the first artist approached to select a stone and make a complementary work. After meeting with the curators and viewing the stones, Cummings decided to make a silver box. His first step in the process was to draw the conceptualized work and to purchase the silver for the project. He used several techniques to make the box, including raising the metal from a flat sheet of silver. He formed the repoussé designs on the sides and lid of the box and used two different dies he had made to stamp an outline around the repoussé design, one V-shaped and the other a design of small dots. He used an older-style die that he had made to stamp a border around the top of the box. He textured the silver lid by striking it repeatedly with a small hammer. He also shaped the hinges for the box and used silver wire for the pins in the hinges. Cummings often uses a heavier wire, such as the type used in clothes hangers, for the pins because the wire is sturdy, lasts a long time, and is tempered. Since this box would be viewed rather than used, he chose silver wire. When he returned to the museum to select a stone for the lid, he chose a large Bisbee turquoise. Cummings had to carefully set the stone because the turquoise did not have a backing and would break more easily than a backed stone. After he bezel-set the stone on the lid, he brought the finished box to the museum.

Rectangular boxes have been made by southwestern jewelers as items for sale as early as 1920. In the late 1990s, Navajo silversmith Ron Bedonie (b. 1967) took the skill to a new level when he created an eight-sided, stemmed container with a lid that was decorated with repoussé along with stamped and chiseled designs. He also made rectangular boxes, miniature containers, and concho belts that incorporated these techniques. His work can be distinguished in part by the addition of a stem to the center base of some containers or at each corner of some boxes.

Gary Reeves (Navajo, b. 1961) and his brother Daniel have received much recognition for the extensive stamp work and, at times, repoussé on the jewelry they each create. Reeves graduated from Tohatchi High School in New Mexico in 1983. He learned silversmithing techniques from his two older brothers, David and Leroy. He has made silver containers, concho belts, earrings, bracelets, buckles, picture frames, yoyos, and letter openers.

Below and opposite: Edison Cummings silver purse with repoussé designs, 2006. This was a Best of Classification winner at the Heard Museum Guild Indian Fair & Market.

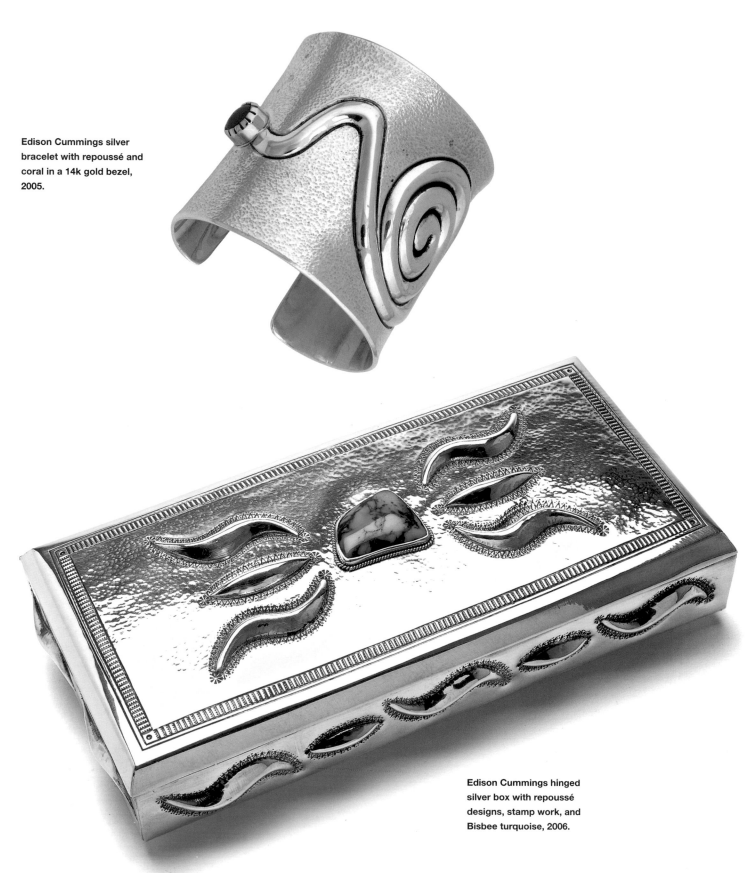

Edison Cummings silver bracelet with repoussé and coral in a 14k gold bezel, 2005.

Edison Cummings hinged silver box with repoussé designs, stamp work, and Bisbee turquoise, 2006.

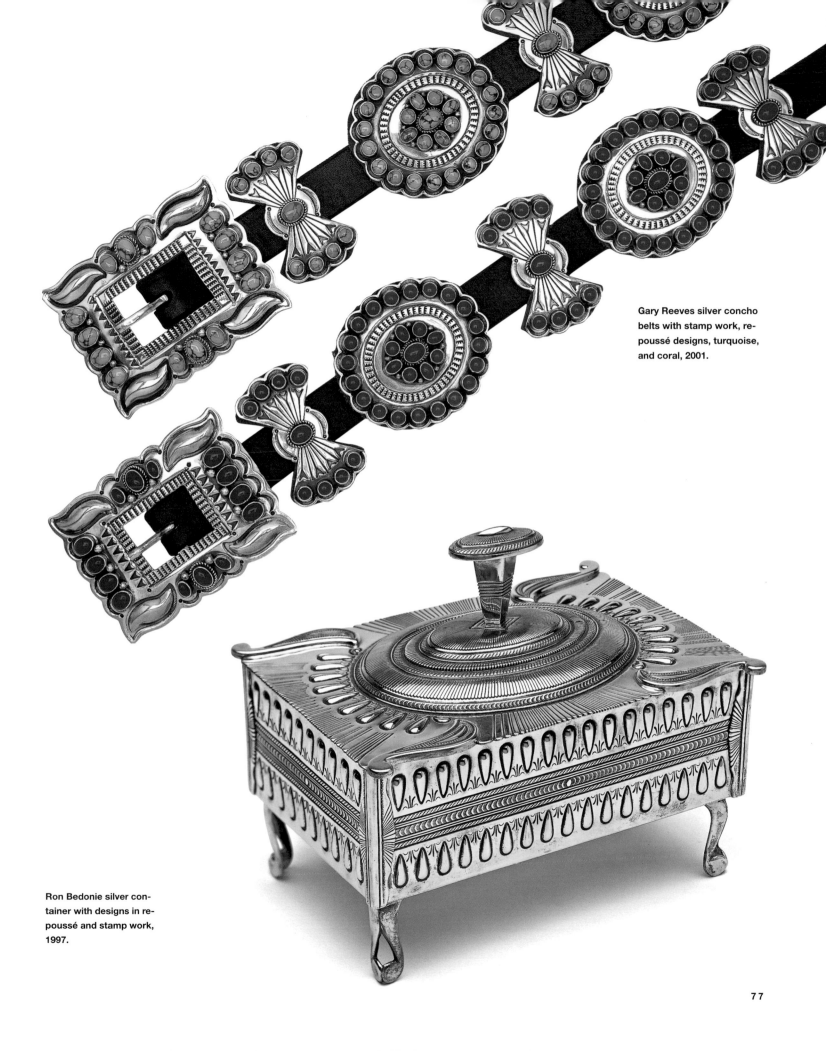

Gary Reeves silver concho belts with stamp work, repoussé designs, turquoise, and coral, 2001.

Ron Bedonie silver container with designs in repoussé and stamp work, 1997.

Texturing the Metal

One typical way jewelers texture the metal is by using a small-head hammer to tap the surface repeatedly in the desired area. Other artists, like Jan Loco, place the silver over rocks and hammer to simulate the texture of the rocks. Norbert Peshlakai and others also use emery paper to provide surface texture. Still other artists use heat to add small bits of silver to change the surface through processes known as granulation or reticulation. All of these techniques alter the surface of the silver, making it bumpy, grainy, or lightly textured like sandpaper.

Silversmith James Faks (Blackfeet/Oneida/Apache, b. 1961) uses hammer-texturing in addition to stamp work to embellish the silver concho belts, earrings, brooches, and purses he makes. Faks, whose birth name is Sinopah, or Red-tail Hawk, was born in northern Montana and learned some basic silver-making skills by watching his father, Shenandoah, although Faks is largely self-taught. Faks also learned how to make tools from his father and other elders whom he credits as having an influence on his work. As a child, Faks traveled to the Southwest with his father and moved there permanently around 1989. He initially lived and worked in Santa Fe but more recently in Cave Creek, Arizona. Faks emphasizes the surface of the silver, making impressions with deep-set stamp work or by hammer texturing.

Kenneth Begay teapot, hammered, with stamp work silver and ironwood, 1963.

Although Faks's work has a classic look, he is not afraid to experiment. In 1999, when the Heard Museum was planning an exhibit "Fashion Fusion" about the convergences of American Indian fashion and mainstream fashion, Faks made a small silver purse with a hammered texture. He has continued to make a few purses each year, but has modified the construction over time. Although the front, back, and lower portion of the purse are formed of hammer-textured sheet silver, Faks uses leather for the ends. He attaches the leather panels by pulling small leather strips through punched holes in the silver purse. He emphasizes simplicity of design in a traditional style but with contemporary lines.

Another accomplished and creative jeweler who initially learned techniques from Norbert Peshlakai is Darrell Jumbo (Navajo, b. 1960). Jumbo was born in Fort Defiance, Arizona, but he retains a close affinity to his family's traditional homeland of Crystal, New Mexico. Following his graduation from Window Rock High School, he enlisted in the Marine Corps for four years and received his honorable discharge in 1983. He attended college at the University of Colorado in Denver where he wanted to study pharmaceuticals and also took a painting class as an elective. After a few

James Faks hammer-textured silver purse, 2006.

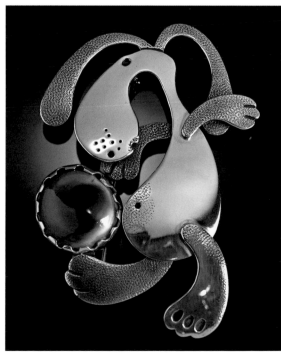

Darrell Jumbo "Dreamweaver," stamp-textured silver brooch with operculum, 2000.

Darrell Jumbo "Proposal Box," textured silver with appliqué, 14k gold and turquoise, 2006. Jumbo placed the silver on a volcanic rock and hit the silver with a leather-tipped hammer to acquire the texture.

Darrell Jumbo hammer-textured and appliquéd silver container with turquoise, "Spring Training," 2006.

80

years at the university, he returned to Fort Defiance. At that time, Jumbo, a nephew of Norbert Peshlakai's wife, Linda, asked his aunt if Peshlakai would teach him metalworking techniques. In 1991, for a period of a month, Peshlakai taught Jumbo basic silversmithing techniques. Jumbo won his first ribbon, a second place prize for a bracelet, in 1994. A few years later, Peshlakai gave Jumbo his artist name, "Elephant Man." Jumbo continues to use an elephant design as his hallmark.

Jumbo's silverwork is whimsical, light, and exquisitely crafted. He has made a variety of brooches of animals that combine reality and fantasy. He uses stamp work and also textures the silver to create contrasts in the silver surface. According to Jumbo, "I enjoy giving forth a variety of techniques: stamp work, fusing, overlay, inlay, reticulation, granulation, texturing, forging, stretching, sinking, etc. My employment with a variety of these techniques on an individual piece brings out its own uniqueness."[23]

In 2005, Jumbo talked with the Heard Museum staff about his interest in making a metalwork object in the shape of a hot dog. With the planned opening for summer 2006 of Heard West in Surprise, Arizona, which was in proximity to the spring training camp for major league baseball teams, the staff contacted Jumbo during the Heard Fair in March to commission the work. Although the staff initially thought that Jumbo was planning to make a brooch, they quickly learned that he was conceptualizing a hotdog-shaped, three-dimensional form. Jumbo proceeded with the work and made "Spring Training." The silver container has four openings on the hammer-textured top to represent the four directions. The container has a bird motif from a petroglyph found in Canyon de Chelly, Arizona, attached as a handle to each of the short ends. Two goats were appliquéd to each of the long sides. Jumbo had positioned the goats to give the appearance that they are going in a circle. They are circling as a part of their training and the black goat is the head trainer. Bezel-set turquoise was added to the lower portion of the container.

Jumbo was one of six artists to be awarded a Southwestern Association of Indian Arts (SWAIA) Fellowship in 2006. This is a prestigious award made by the organization whose annual event is the Indian Market held in Santa Fe each August. Jumbo indicated that he plans to purchase jewelry equipment, including a dremel and stone cutting and polishing tools, with his award. According to Jumbo, "As long as art has no boundaries, and with a grace of balance and beauty, I'm free to achieve my dreams and ambition in metal."[24]

Silversmith Jan Loco (Apache, b. 1955) textures the silver jewelry she makes to resemble the rough rocks around her home in New Mexico. She creates texture in the jewelry by placing a sheet of silver over a rock and hammering the metal repeatedly. Loco sometimes looks for an hour or more until she finds the surface she wants to transfer to the silver.

Loco began to seek information about her Apache heritage when she learned as an adult that she was adopted. Chiricahua Apache sculptor and painter Allan Houser helped her to find out about her family. She learned that she was descended from Apache leader Chief Loco. Jan Loco began to use imagery from her Apache heritage and the natural world in her jewelry. One of the images is the four-point morning star, which she often uses in earrings and necklaces. Other images that Loco uses and that often inspire her brooches are the rabbits, turtles, coyotes, and butterflies she sees in New Mexico and spirals and designs inspired by southwestern petroglyphs.

Loco further enhances the texture of the metal by polishing the hammer-textured surfaces with several grades of steel wool. She uses a white diamond compound to achieve the textured surface as well. Loco uses hand tools—shears, hammers, files, and other tools—and does not use electric tools. The process of hammering has taken its toil on her small frame, and Loco has had periods of time when she has been unable to work because of injuries resulting from the rigors of constant hammering.

Norbert Peshlakai has taught his children, Natasha and Aaron, metalworking and jewelry techniques. Natasha (b. 1981) learned basic silversmithing techniques such as stamp work and soldering as a young girl. By age twelve, she won her first award at the Indian Market in Santa Fe. She has continued to explore other silversmithing techniques, some of which she applies to miniature silver

Darrell Jumbo at the Heard Museum Guild Indian Fair & Market, 2002.

Jan Loco, "Morningstar Necklace" of textured silver and obsidian, 1990.

seed jars, the construction of which she learned from her father. Like her father, Natasha employs stamp work and hammer texturing to embellish her work.

Some concepts require creative measures. In order to attach the hair design to a figure on one of her miniature lidded jars, Natasha drilled a hole on each side of the figure and pulled the wire through, making the wire hair attachments taut. This was so successful that she only had to add a small bit of solder and reduced the risk of melting the fine wire she had attached.

Jan Loco hammer-textured silver spiral pin, 2000.

Larry Golsh hammer-textured silver and 18k gold bracelet, 2004.

Natasha Peshlakai textured silver jar with 14k gold, 2002.

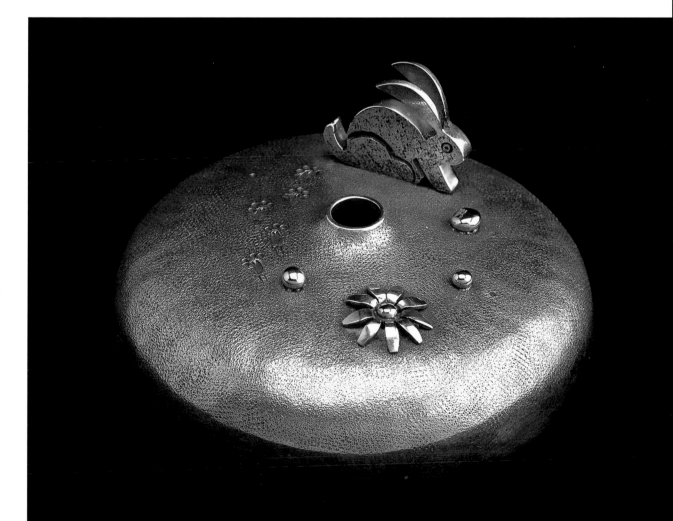

Darrell Jumbo "The Queen's Pot," miniature teapot with stamp-textured and appliquéd silver, coral, and sugilite, 2005.

Natasha Peshlakai hammer-textured silver jar with coral and 14k gold, 2004.

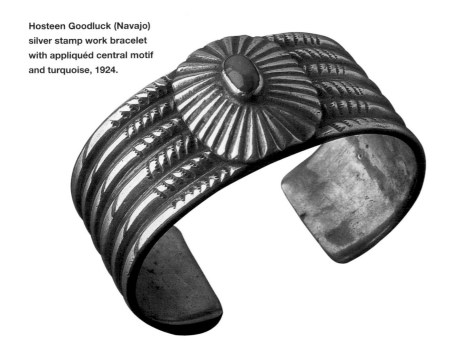

Hosteen Goodluck (Navajo)
silver stamp work bracelet
with appliquéd central motif
and turquoise, 1924.

Appliqué

Appliqué, one of the basic silversmithing techniques, is a process of adding a metal element to the surface of another metal element. This is accomplished by using heat to fuse a decorative metal element onto a metal surface.

Clarence Lee (Navajo, b. 1952) and his son Russell Lee (Navajo, b. 1976) create pictorial designs cut out in silver or copper and appliquéd to a plate of silver that might form a bracelet or a complex container. Clarence is a self-taught artist who has passed on the techniques of jewelry making to Russell. Clarence first developed the storyteller themes around 1973, when he developed his first sheepherder bracelet. The concept developed unintentionally when Clarence sawed a dog shape out of silver plate, appliquéd it to another plate of silver, and made it into a ring.

Today, father and son work on some jewelry collaboratively and others independently. Both

Clarence Lee bracelet with
appliquéd designs in silver
and copper and inlay motif
of white shell, coral,
turquoise, and jet, 1989.

Clarence and Russell Lee music box of silver with appliquéd motifs of silver, copper, and brass, 2006. The music box plays "Amazing Grace." It was purchased at the Heard Museum Guild Indian Fair & Market.

Robert Taylor bolo tie in 14k gold with appliquéd design, 2005.

men use copper for designs accents, adding an outline of Monument Valley or other landmark to the storyteller themes. Around 1979 or 1980, Clarence began appliquéing 14k gold motifs to his jewelry. The different colors of metal create a striking contrast and, along with the appliqué technique, provide depth to the figurative scenes.

Robert Taylor (Navajo, b. 1961) also creates scenes of Navajo life in silver and gold and in silver motifs that are first cut out of the metal and then appliquéd to another metal surface. Taylor's "storyteller" jewelry is created in bracelets, pendants, buckles, concho belts, and other jewelry forms. As a young boy, Taylor spent summer vacations tending his grandmother's sheep. Storytelling was something that he learned from his father, Carl, who also taught him how to make jewelry. Taylor started silversmithing at age ten by buffing jewelry made by his brothers and sisters. Taylor uses de-

Robert Taylor 14k gold appliquéd bracelet and bear pendant, 2005.

Perry Shorty bracelet with appliquéd silver drops, silver wire, and hand-twisted silver wire and stamp work, 2001.

tailed designs to tell stories of Navajo life.

Working in an older, traditional style, silversmith Perry Shorty appliqués silver drops, silver wire and hand-twisted wire as decorative elements. He combines the appliqué with stamp work, creating an overall complex and highly decorative design. Shorty's work is distinguished by its resemblance to early silver jewelry and his use of silver ingots.

Overlay

In the overlay technique a jeweler uses two sheets of metal, cutting out the design in one layer and laying it over the other. In silver overlay, the lower sheet is often oxidized with liver of sulphur to darken it. Some jewelers also texture the lower sheet with stamp or awl work.

Silver overlay began as a collaborative effort between the Museum of Northern Arizona and the Hopi tribe after World War II in an attempt to develop a distinctive jewelry form for Hopi silversmiths. Paul Saufkie (1898–1998) was one of the

Paul Saufkie silver overlay buckle, early 1960s.

first jewelers to accomplish the technique, and he along with Fred Kabotie taught veterans the overlay techniques from 1947–51.[25] Today, many Hopi jewelers continue to use overlay, but it is also made by other contemporary jewelers regardless of tribal affiliation.

Victor Coochwytewa (Hopi, b. 1922) was a student of Paul Saufkie and Fred Kabotie's jewelry-making class taught at Oraibi, Arizona. Coochwytewa had returned home from serving in the U.S. Army in World War II. He added a new dimension to his overlay technique by adding texture to the oxidized background. He was also one of the first Hopi artists to use gold in overlay instead of silver in the 1970s.

Michael Kabotie (Hopi, b. 1942) finds inspiration for his jewelry and paintings in ancient mural paintings of Awatovi, the rich graphics of the Sikyatki ruins, and petroglyphs in the Four Corners area of Arizona, New Mexico, Utah, and Colorado. Kabotie's jewelry designs are abstract renderings often executed in silver overlay and at times in gold. Kabotie works on both his paintings and jewelry, sometimes in simultaneous projects. In 2004, he created two large-scale drawings of two by twelve feet of abstract designs and made small-scale silver overlay renditions of them after working with the Museum of Northern Arizona on a project to document murals in the northern part of the state.

Kabotie first learned about jewelry making while he was still in high school, when Wally Sekayumptewa of Hotevilla, Arizona, showed him the technique. He was also guided by his cousins McBride and Mark Lomayestewa and Walter Polelonema. Kabotie's distinctive designs translate well in the overlay technique. He signs both his paintings and his jewelry with his Hopi name, Lomawywesa. Because of his emphasis on mural design, Kabotie's jewelry is distinctive. In addition to silver, he also creates similar patterns in gold.

Another Hopi jeweler who works with silver overlay is Bernard Dawahoya. Born at the village of Songoopavi in 1937, Dawahoya began making artwork as a boy, including carved sandstone, painted rocks, and sand drawings. By the time he was nineteen, he was accomplished at katsina carving and painting, but his primary interest was silversmithing.

Above: Victor Coochwytewa silver overlay bracelet with a design of a pahlik-mana, 1970s.

Below: Victor Coochwytewa silver overlay necklace with a design of stepped clouds and rain, 1970s.

Michael Kabotie
silver overlay
bracelet, 1997.

Michael Kabotie 14k gold
and silver overlay necklace
and bracelet, 2006.

Michael Kabotie at his
booth at the 2001 Heard
Museum Guild Indian Fair &
Market.

Bernard Dawahoya silver overlay jar, 2001.

Dawahoya makes a range of jewelry, but he also creates distinctive forms in the shape of silver jars and vases in silver overlay. Some of these are fashioned in the low-shoulder pottery shape that was traditionally Sikyatki pottery. The shape was popularized by the Tewa potter Nampeyo in the early 1900s, and the form continues to be made by contemporary potters in clay and by some jewelers in silver or other metals.

Dawahoya was a business entrepreneur with Wayne Sekaquaptewa when the two men opened a shop in 1960 in a side room of radio station KOY's transmitter station in northeast Phoenix. During this time, Dawahoya perfected his silvermaking skills under the tutelage of silversmith Harry Sakyesva. After three years, the men moved the

Gary and Elsie Yoyokie silver overlay bolo tie with 14k gold appliqué, 1994.

Gary and Elsie Yoyokie silver overlay bolo tie with 14k gold appliqué, 1997.

Roderick Tenorio holds his
prize-winning concho belt
at the Heard Museum Guild
Indian Fair & Market, 2001.

business to Kykotsmovi, Arizona, where they
taught other young Hopi men to make silver jewelry. In 1966, Dawahoya left the business and began to devote time to his personal artwork.[26]

Jason Takala (Hopi, b. 1955) was born in Songoopavi Village, Arizona, but attended high school
in Woodstock, Vermont. He learned silversmithing
at the Hopi Guild under Alde Qumayintewa, also
of Songoopavi, during summer breaks from high
school. Around 1979, Qumayintewa taught Takala
how to cut silver, solder, and polish. In exchange,
Takala shared design concepts with Qumayintewa.
From 1980–85, Takala studied with Scottsdale jeweler Pierre Touraine. Although Takala makes concho belts and silver and gold jewelry using the
overlay technique, he also specializes in silver seed
jars for which he has won many awards.

Elsie (Navajo, b. 1951) and Gary Yoyokie
(Hopi, b. 1953) create highly detailed silver overlay
jewelry with accents in 14k gold. Gary was born in
Third Mesa, Arizona, but went to school at
Phoenix Indian High School and later attended
Northern Arizona University in Flagstaff. When he
was twelve, he helped Wayne Sekaquaptewa at the
Hopi Craft Shop by sweeping and doing other
tasks. He learned some basic silversmithing skills

Left: Roderick Tenorio bolo
tie in silver overlay with
Number 8 Turquoise, 1994.

Below: Roderick Tenorio
14k gold overlay concho
belt, 2001.

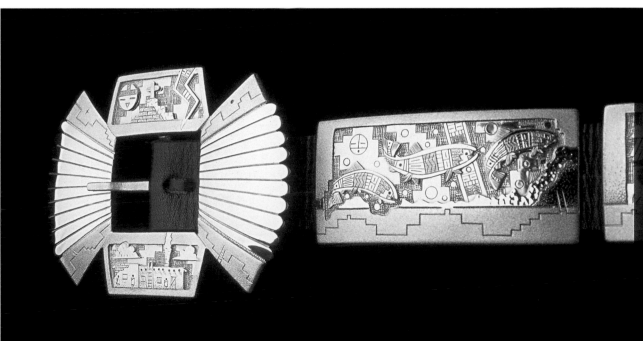

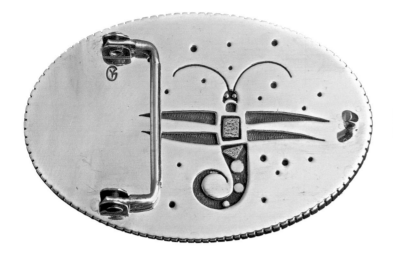

Yazzie Johnson and Gail Bird buckle of a Mimbres-style dragonfly in mist in silver overlay with appliqué of tufa-cast 18k gold and 18k gold drops for the eyes, 2004.

Lace agate buckle front.

Yazzie Johnson and Gail Bird buckle with a silver overlay design based on early Hopi pottery from the village of Sikyatki. The eyes are 18k gold drops and a circle was cut out of a sheet of tufa-cast 18k gold and appliquéd in the center, 2005.

Deschutes jasper buckle front.

Yazzie Johnson and Gail Bird buckle reverses in silver overlay with 18k gold appliqué. From top: Parrot design with stars, 2004; running antelope, 2005; and bird and cloud design, 2003.

Buckle fronts of Deschutes jasper, Paiute Sage jasper, and Parrel Plume jasper.

from Sekaquaptewa. He and Elsie met during high school, and Elsie learned jewelry techniques by assisting Gary. Gary designs the jewelry that he and Elsie create together, and many of the designs reflect elements of Hopi culture.

In 2001, Roderick Tenorio (Santo Domingo, b. 1955) won the Best of Classification award for jewelry at the Heard Museum Guild Indian Fair & Market for a concho belt made in 14k gold overlay. He had won the Best of Show award at the Gallup Inter-Tribal Ceremonial the prior year. Tenorio grew up in Santo Domingo where, by age seven, he was helping his grandparents make jewelry by breaking olive shells (Olividae) with a hammer and by cutting them with the blade edge of a pair of pliers. After high school, Tenorio joined the U.S. Army, where he served for three years. Around 1978, he began making jewelry, initially out of brass and later of silver. He studied sculpture while a student at the Institute of American Indian Arts in Santa Fe from 1979 to 1981 and became more interested in jewelry while taking some jewelry classes at IAIA. While working in sculpture, Tenorio learned "to make curves like waves" by using a technique of tapping a stone gently with the sculpting tools. He applied those same skills to his metalwork to accomplish curved lines. He makes many of his own tools, forming small chisels out of concrete nails or files that he alters. He decided to set his jewelry apart from other Santo Domingo jewelers by working in overlay, a technique rarely used by other jewelers at Santo Domingo. He further distinguished his work by stamping the background, or the lower plate of silver, rather than just texturing it.

Yazzie Johnson and Gail Bird have used the overlay technique, which they refer to as "underlay" when used on the reverse side of buckles or other bezel-set stones. They were inspired by Charles Loloma's application of stone inlay designs on ring and bracelet interiors. Their buckles incorporate naturally patterned stones that they select for their distinctive landscapes, sky and earth formations, or complex abstract patterns. The metal surface is sometimes accented with 18k gold appliqué shapes.

Above: Yazzie Johnson and Gail Bird Buckle in silver overlay, 2005.

Below: Duane Maktima buckle in silver overlay with 14k gold, sugilite, black jade, and faustite, 1997.

Jason Takala silver overlay lidded container, 2003.

Duane Maktima silver container with lid in silver overlay and opalized ironstone, lapis lazuli, calkacydirite, and turquoise, 2002.

STONE PATTERNING

Near right: Kenneth Begay fabricated silver bracelet with stamp work, hand-twisted wire and bezel-set coral, 1975.

Far right: Roger Skeet (Navajo) fabricated silver bracelet with stamp work and bezel-set turquoise and jet, 1950s.

Emphasizing the Metal and Stonework

Southwestern jewelers have long appreciated and emphasized combinations of stones and metalwork. Native garnets, petrified wood, jet, and a variety of turquoise have been used as settings for silver jewelry. In the 1970s, when gold began to be used more frequently, combining it with turquoise was thought to be innovative as well as appealing to jewelry collectors. Some collectors in the past preferred the silver and turquoise combinations and many continue to do so today. Through the innovative use of a wide range of stones that include picture jaspers and agates incorporated into the jewelry of Yazzie Johnson and Gail Bird, Shawn Bluejacket, Mike Bird-Romero, and others, the combinations today are limitless.

Yazzie Johnson (Navajo, b. 1946) and Gail Bird (Santo Domingo/Laguna, b. 1949) began making jewelry in the early 1970s.[1] Their early work was in red or yellow brass as well as silver. They distinguished their work early on by the unusual assortment of stones that they used, including calibrated jaspers, blood stones, and agates chosen for the pictorial patterns and the way the stones looked with brass. In 1972, Johnson and Bird attended the University of Colorado in Boulder where Johnson studied art and Bird studied humanities. Johnson is largely a self-taught artist who learned many techniques by referring to John Adair's 1944 book *Navajo and Pueblo Silversmiths*. Although he and Bird discussed designs and materials when Johnson began making jewelry, their collaboration intensified in the late 1970s when Bird became more actively involved in designing the work.

In 1979, Johnson and Bird created their first thematic belt, and with one exception, they have made one annually for the Indian Market held each August in Santa Fe. In 1981, they won Best of Show at Indian Market for the belt they entered into the competition. A distinguishing feature of their work is the design on the underside of buckles or clasps and satellites in necklaces. They were inspired by the work of Charles Loloma, who added designs in turquoise or other stones to the interior of bracelets or rings and the reverse sides of

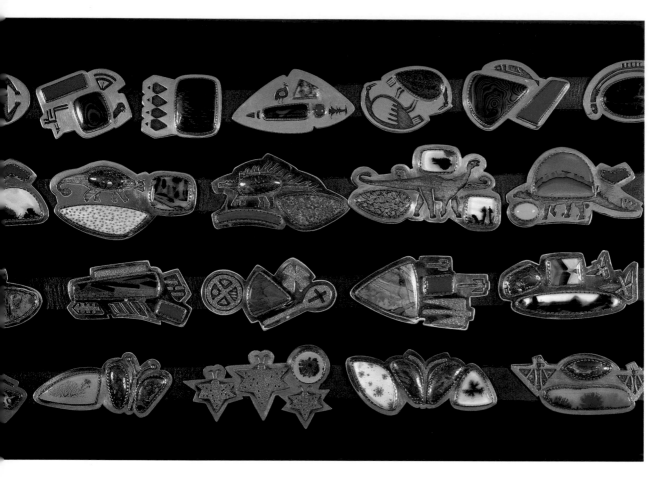

Yazzie Johnson and Gail Bird detail of thematic belts.
From top: "Mimbres Black and White Belt," 1984, petrified wood, psilomelane, coral, Tyrone turquoise, Mahogonite, silver overlay and stamp work, and 14k gold appliqué. "Dinosaur Belt," 2002, coral, turquoise, Montana agate, Yowah opal, petrified palmwood, dinosaur bone, Sleeping Beauty turquoise, silver overlay, and 18k tufa-cast gold appliqué. "All Things Hopi Belt," 2005, Montana agate, coral, brecciated jasper, aggregate agate, Morrisonite, Yowah opal, and silver with 18k tufa-cast gold appliqué. "Butterfly Belt," 2001, Montana agate, Yowah opal, dendritic agate, moss agate, silver overlay, and 18k tufa-cast gold appliqué.

buckles and pendants. Whereas Loloma created his designs on the reverse side in stones, Johnson and Bird create their "underlay" designs in metal.

Early in their careers in the late 1970s, Johnson and Bird initiated jewelry ideas that they have continued to use. One was to create earrings of different shapes and sizes. The idea evolved into earrings of different but complementary materials as well as shapes. Throughout their careers, they have continued to develop innovative designs and use new materials.

Shawn Bluejacket (Loyal Shawnee, b. 1962) emphasizes the metalwork in her jewelry but also incorporates unusual stones. When Bluejacket was a young child, her family moved to Auckland, New Zealand, where her father worked as a geologist. After high school, she studied fashion design at the Brooks College of Design in Long Beach, California, from 1984 to 1986. She also studied with Lane Coulter from 1989 to 1990 and Duane Mak-

tima from 1991 to 1992 at the Institute of American Indian Arts in Santa Fe. Bluejacket's use of exotic stones may in part derive from her father's interest in stones.

Bluejacket creates hollow-form, constructed sculptural jewelry. She prefers a matte texture to a highly polished one and uses etching to texture the surfaces. For Bluejacket, the metalwork is the most important aspect of the jewelry. Her lapidary skills allow her to shape the stones to fit her metalwork designs. Bluejacket, like Johnson and Bird, emphasizes asymmetry in earrings. Her jewelry is light and delicate, and the etchings on the metal have the same lightness. One method she uses is photo etching, a process of scanning a computer image or photograph onto the metal.

In 2001, Bluejacket bought a parcel of uncut opals from Lightning Ridge, Australia. She undertook the task of cutting and polishing with Japanese sandpaper one very large black opal

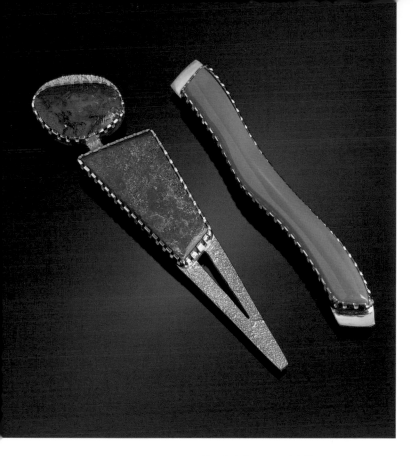

Yazzie Johnson and Gail
Bird lapis lazuli, Yowah
opal, and 18k gold tufa-cast
pin, 2004, and pink coral
and 18k gold pin, 2000.

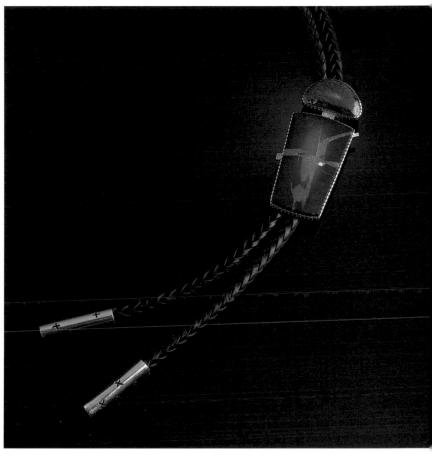

Yazzie Johnson and Gail
Bird bolo tie of Yowah opal,
brecciated jasper, and 18k
gold, 2001.

Yazzie Johnson and Gail
Bird Boulder opal and 18k
gold bolo tie, 2002.

from the group. During the process, Bluejacket looked at the opal several times with a gemologist, who used a gem microscope to determine if continued polishing would reveal more color in the stone. Excessive polishing would have taken the stone beyond its best color. It took Bluejacket approximately fourteen hours to cut and polish the 90.5-carat opal, the largest she has used in jewelry to date.

In recent years, Bluejacket has made miniature metal containers that she shapes into small houses, flowerpots, and other forms. She paints these in bright colors. For a 2004 Heard Museum North gala, she made a small salt and pepper shaker set and used sections of coral and lapis lazuli along with silver for the tripod base.

Although Veronica Poblano (b. 1951) is the daughter of Zuni carver and mosaic artist Leo Poblano, she too is largely a self-taught jeweler.

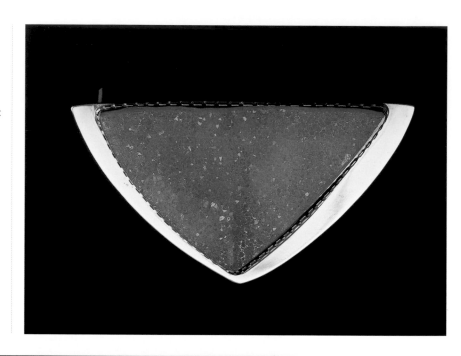

Above: Yazzie Johnson and Gail Bird pin of drusy chrysocolla and 14k gold, 1999.

Left: Yazzie Johnson and Gail Bird. From top: Silver mabe pearl, black star sapphire, and 18k gold earrings, 1999. Yowah opal and 18k gold earrings, 1999. Lapis lazuli, dinosaur bone, and 18k gold earrings, 2001. Coral, garnet, and 18k gold earrings, 2000. Chrysoprase, Mexican lace agate, and 18k gold earrings, 2001. Tangerine and blue chalcedony and 18k gold earrings, 2002.

Shawn Bluejacket necklace
of drusy quartz, chryso-
prase, chrysocolla, opal,
South Sea pearl, amethyst,
ammonite, silver, and 14k
gold, 1999.

Shawn Bluejacket necklace
and earrings of lavender
chalcedony and 18k gold,
2002.

Shawn Bluejacket necklace
of black opal and 18k gold,
2001.

Mike Bird-Romero fabricated bracelet and earrings of coral, jet, and silver, 2001.

Mike Bird-Romero fabricated bracelets of turquoise, lace agate, and fossilized palmwood, 2002.

Mike Bird-Romero fabricated pins of silver, turquoise, and discoidal turquoise beads, 2002.

Veronica Poblano fabricated necklace and ring of red and black coral and silver, 2006.

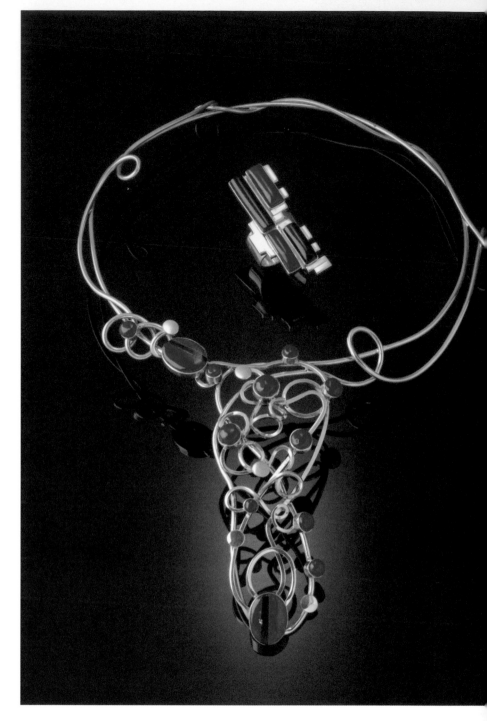

She began experimenting with jewelry making around the age of ten and by age thirteen was making jewelry on her own. In the 1970s, when Poblano was in her early twenties, she developed a series of inlay pins based on Walt Disney characters. She began to specialize in stone shaping and multistone inlay and in recent years has distinguished her work by the interplay of contrasting colors, such as the rich purple of sugilite and the apple green of gaspeite. After making jewelry for

about twenty years, Poblano wanted to pursue a new avenue and decided to go to cosmetology school. Those teachings, which included learning about the color wheel and primary and secondary color combinations, changed Poblano's perspective on color choices and resulted in a new color palette for her jewelry.

In 1999, Poblano converted part of her home in Zuni into a gallery she shares with her daughter Jovana, who makes bead and stone jewelry. Always

one to experiment and grow, Poblano attended the
Revere Academy of Jewelry Arts in San Francisco
in 2004 and 2005 to learn new techniques and develop new ideas for her jewelry. She selected different classes from the broad curriculum at the
Revere Academy and chose to learn the technique
of granulation and how to make different types of
clasps. Poblano brings this knowledge and her own
experiences to the jewelry she creates.

Duane Maktima (Laguna/Hopi, b. 1954) be-

came interested in creating jewelry when he was a
student at Northern Arizona University in Flagstaff.
His interest increased when he was selected, along
with two other American Indian artists, to be an
intern artist in residence at the Museum of Northern Arizona in 1975. The museum collection was
extensive and inspirational to the young jeweler.

After earning his bachelor of arts degree, Maktima moved to his mother's home of Laguna
Pueblo. He returned to NAU and earned a master

Vernon Haskie coral and
14k gold bolo tie, 2002. This
won Best of Classification
at the Heard Museum Guild
Indian Fair & Market.

Veronica Poblano at the
2006 Heard Museum Guild
Indian Fair & Market.

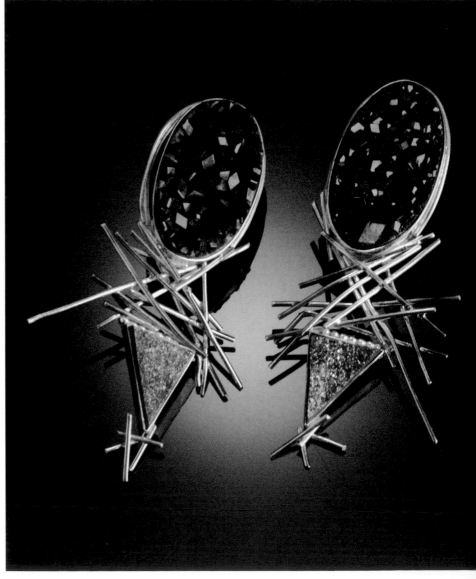

Veronica Poblano earrings
of drusy garnet, drusy
pyrite, and silver, 2002.

Shawn Bluejacket salt and pepper shakers and stand of lapis lazuli, coral, silver, and 14k gold, 2003.

of arts degree in 1982. In 1990, he began teaching at the Institute of American Indian Arts in Santa Fe, and in 1998, he began the Pueblo V Design Studio where he taught metalsmithing techniques to young jewelers, including Myron Panteah and Kee Yazzie.

Maktima uses the overlay technique to create abstract images in silver and meshes them with unusual stones. He has developed a signature jewelry pattern using rosarita, white shell, jet, and opal for pendants, bracelets, and necklaces.

Richard Chavez (San Felipe, b. 1949) initially trained as an architect at the University of New Mexico in Albuquerque and worked as a draftsman for a period of time after graduation in 1975. During this time, he found jeweler's tools at his parents' home when he was clearing out their belongings. He became interested in jewelry making and began to teach himself the techniques. Chavez fabricates jewelry and also cuts and polishes his own stones. His inlay work has become increasingly complex as he incorporates complementary colored stones in intricate patterns.

Mosaic on Shell or Wood

The tradition of creating mosaic patterns on stone, shell, or wood is centuries old in the Southwest. The Hohokam of central and southern present-day Arizona inlaid cut sections of stones onto shell pendants and bracelets using tree pitch as an adhesive. By the late 1800s, Hopi women were wearing earrings made of cottonwood with turquoise mosaic patterns. During the Depression and the years following, jewelers from Santo Domingo Pueblo created gypsum bead necklaces with mosaic patterned pendants in the shape of birds. The mosaics on these "thunderbird" necklaces were made with real turquoise chips, but pieces of car batteries or record albums were often used instead of jet to form the black bases. Plastics from toothbrush handles and other ready-made items were often used instead of coral for red.

Santo Domingo jeweler Angie Owen (b. 1945) recalls helping her mother, Clara Reano, make thunderbird necklaces when Owen was a child. Her father, Joe I. Reano, and grandfather, Isidro Reano, were jewelers as well. They made heishi-shaped-and-cut beads of turquoise or shell for which Santo Domingo jewelers are well known.

In the early 1970s, Santo Domingo Pueblo jewelers led by Owen and others revived the concept of mosaics on shell or wood. While on a trip to Tucson, collector and author Oscar Branson showed Owen examples of prehistoric mosaic jewelry. When Owen began creating mosaics, she initially added patterns to only a portion of a shell such as the tops of small bivalves that she made into earrings or pendants. By the mid-1980s, she was creating complex mosaic patterns over shells that she had cut and shaped to form bangle-style bracelets. At times, she selected shells with natural contours that enhanced the mosaic patterns. Owen primarily uses turquoise and adds color contrasts of varying hues of natural shells, coral, jet, and lapis lazuli.

Owen begins by cutting and shaping the shell or wood into the desired shape. She next decides upon a color pattern and cuts the stones into small pieces that she adheres to the shell or wood base with an adhesive. After the adhesive sets and dries, she grinds the entire surface and then sands using increasingly finer grades of sandpaper. For the final step, Owen uses a buffer to polish the entire surface of the mosaic jewelry. Owen's work is distinguished by the complex patterns and detailed mosaics.

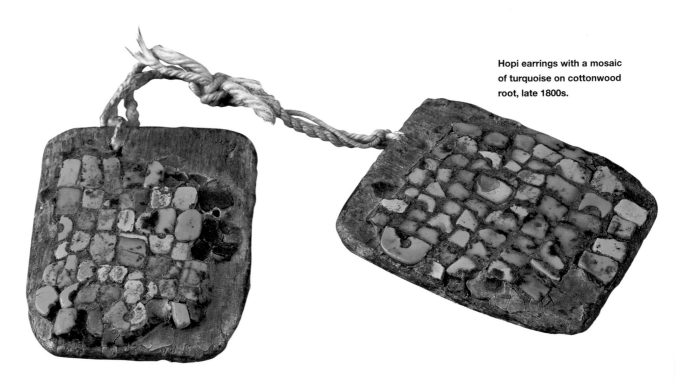

Hopi earrings with a mosaic of turquoise on cottonwood root, late 1800s.

Above: Angie Reano Owen 2003 pendant and 1986 bracelet and ring of turquoise, jet, shell, spiny oyster, coral, and lapis lazuli.

Left: Angie Reano Owen shell bracelet with a mosaic of coral, lapis lazuli, spiny oyster shell, and other shells, 2003.

Right: Angie Owen at the Heard Museum Guild Indian Fair & Market, 2006.

Charlene Sanchez Reano reversible necklace of black-lip mother of pearl, spiny oyster shell, yellow-lip mother of pearl, and abalone, 2006. This necklace won Best of Division at the 2006 Heard Museum Guild Indian Fair & Market.

Angie Owen's brother, Frank Reano, and his wife, Charlene, have also distinguished their mosaic jewelry. For the 2006 Heard Museum Guild Indian Fair & Market, Charlene Reano made a reversible necklace of mosaic on shell. The color choices of the black-lipped mother of pearl contrasting with the lighter shell colors make a visually dramatic work. The Reano family members continue to develop intriguing designs with intricate mosaic.

Charlene Sanchez Reano (San Felipe, b. 1960) met her husband Frank (Santo Domingo, b. 1962) when they were students in high school in Highlands, New Mexico. Charlene studied art during high school but actually learned jewelry techniques from Frank's parents, Clara and Joe I. Reano. Initially, Charlene worked with Clara to make heishi necklaces, and later Charlene and Frank worked with his sister, Angie Owen. For the past ten years, Charlene has been designing her own jewelry,

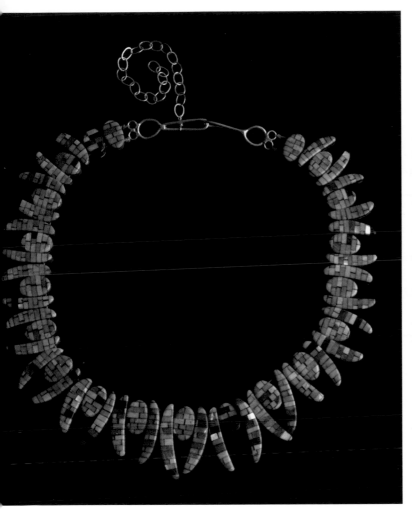 

Charlene Sanchez Reano necklace and reverse, of
turquoise, black-lip mother-of-pearl, spiny oyster
shell, yellow-lip mother-of-pearl, and abalone, 2006.

Charlie Bird belt of silver, gold-lip mother of pearl, black-lip mother of pearl, abalone, white shell, coral, and jet, 1994.

Detail of Charlie Bird belt.

although she has been making jewelry for over twenty-six years. She often has a new design in mind for two or three years before actually creating the work. Such was the case with the reversible necklace. She conceptualizes the design and imagines the colors and materials that will best illustrate the idea. The family members also talk about designs and ways to improve an idea or create something new and make frequent trips to California to get the shells for their jewelry.

Charlie Bird (Santo Domingo/Laguna, b. 1943) also creates a distinctive style of mosaic patterning. His mosaics are linear in form and were inspired by the architecture of Chaco Canyon. In the 1970s, Angie and her husband at the time, Don Owen, encouraged Bird to try making mosaics. Bird had been helping the couple in their jewelry business and had seen the mosaics Owen was making. Bird learned to make mosaics through experimentation, teaching himself the techniques. A trip to Chaco Canyon was inspirational for his work, which reflects the patterns in stone and the passageways that aligned on a grid system so that looking through one results in looking through several others.

Stone Inlay

For decades, Zuni jewelers have been masters at stone inlay. Rich color contrasts of turquoise, coral, and jet continue in contemporary works but might be augmented by the blues of lapis lazuli, purples of sugilite, and colors of other recently used stones. When John Adair conducted his classic research in 1938, many Zuni jewelers were inlaying patterns of dragonflies and knifewings that were set onto silver plates.[2] In the 1930s, the inlay work was often accomplished by Zuni artists while the silverwork was frequently done by Navajo silversmiths.

Some traders living at Zuni, such as C. G. Wallace, provided homes for Navajo silversmiths who developed the silver foundations for the Zuni lapidary work.[3] Contemporary jewelers who undertake inlay are gen-

Above: Zuni knifewing pin of turquoise, coral, spiny oyster shell, white shell, jet, and silver, 1930s.

Below: John Gordon Leek inlaid dragonfly pin of turquoise, coral, jet, and silver, 1940s.

erally accomplished at both lapidary and metalwork.

By the mid-1920s some Zuni lapidarists were also setting stones into silver compartments in a technique that has been referred to as *channel work*. In this process, the metal form determines the layout of the stones, whereas in inlay, shells or stones are inset into other stones. In the 1950s and decades that followed, this became a more frequently employed jewelry technique by Zuni jewelers than stone inlay. Today Zuni jewelers continue to make channel-work jewelry, although other southwestern jewelers undertake the process as well.

By 1975, Charles Loloma had created bracelets with inset stones, often of varying heights, that fit side by side in rows. Loloma had revolutionized yet another form of stone inlay. He and his niece Verma Nequatewa (Sonwai) also developed complex stone patterning that they used in a landscape surface such as that of buckles or bolo ties. Many contemporary jewelers have been inspired to incorporate these concepts into their jewelry. All of the stone-patterning techniques discussed here are used by jewelers today.

Jeweler and longtime Scottsdale resident Jesse Monongya (Navajo, b. 1952) creates lapis lazuli skies that hold full opal moons surrounded by constellations and inlays them in buckles, bracelets, and pendants.[4] His intricate inlay incorporates a multitude of precious and semiprecious stones.

Monongya was raised by his Navajo grandmother and was brought up with the stars, moon, and sun. He remembers his life vividly as a young boy living in a traditional Navajo home, a hogan. He spent many hours looking at the stars in the vast Arizona night sky through the opening in the roof that allowed the smoke from the fire to escape. His grandmother told the seasons by the big dipper and talked to Monongya about the constellations. Much of those teachings are reflected in his jewelry.

In 1974, after returning from military service in Vietnam, Monongya learned to make jewelry by watching his father, renowned artist Preston Monongye. He remembers studying the movements of his father's hands as he made jewelry. Whereas the elder was accomplished at manipulat-

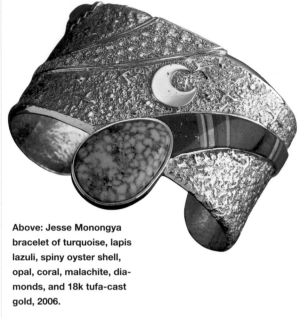

Above: Jesse Monongya bracelet of turquoise, lapis lazuli, spiny oyster shell, opal, coral, malachite, diamonds, and 18k tufa-cast gold, 2006.

Above: Jesse Monongya bracelet of diamond, sugilite, coral, turquoise, fossilized ivory, lapis lazuli, and 18k gold, 2002.

Below: Raymond Yazzie "Blessings," inlaid bracelet of turquoise, coral, lapis lazuli, shell, jet, and 18k gold, 2003. This was a Best of Classification winner at the Heard Museum Guild Indian Fair & Market.

ing the metal, Jesse excelled at metalsmithing techniques as well as the art of delicate stone inlay. In order to learn how to make stone inlay, Monongya studied jewelry by accomplished stoneworkers like jeweler Lee Yazzie, who did some of the fine inlay work for Monongya's father. Through experimentation, great care, and diligence, Monongya began to accomplish complex stone inlay. In 1975, he started to focus on a full-time career as a jeweler.

The process of inlay requires expert technical skill. Monongya polishes each stone separately after it is inlaid because the stones have varying degrees of hardness or softness. After each stone is polished, Monongya covers the stone with a layer of hot wax to protect it while he polishes the others. Monongya's inlaid jewelry was a departure from 1970s traditional southwestern jewelry that featured quality turquoise in silver settings. Monongya took advantage of the range of turquoise available, but like Charles Loloma and Preston Monongye, Jesse forged his own path and

Carolyn Bobelu necklace of channelwork silver with turquoise, coral, spiny oyster shell, mother of pearl, and jet, 1983. This necklace won Carolyn Bobelu the Indian Arts and Crafts Association award of Artist of the Year in 1983.

Left: Edison Cummings
inlay necklace and buckle
of ironwood, turquoise, jet,
coral, and silver, 2006.

Below: Edison Cummings
inlay bracelet of ironwood,
fossilized ivory, turquoise,
coral, and silver, 2006.

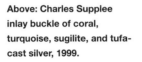

Above: Charles Supplee
inlay buckle of coral,
turquoise, sugilite, and tufa-
cast silver, 1999.

Above: Carl and Irene Clark
fine inlay bracelet of
turquoise, coral, jet, shell,
lapis lazuli, and stamp-work
silver, 1990s.

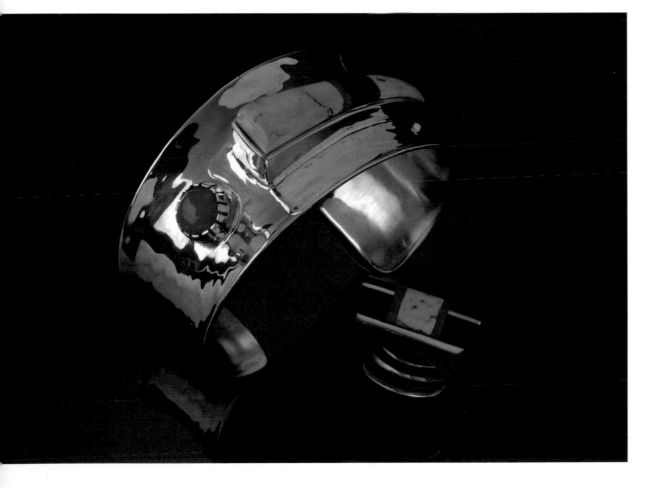

Left: Edison Cummings
bracelet of turquoise, coral,
jet, 14k gold, and silver,
2006, and ring of ironwood,
coral, turquoise, and silver,
2006.

Richard Chavez ring and earrings of lapis lazuli, coral, turquoise, and 18k gold, 2006.

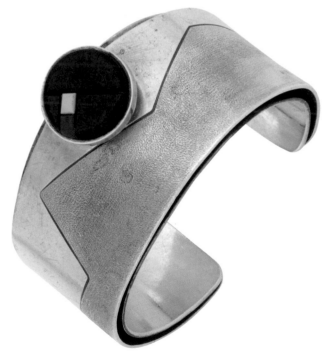

Richard Chavez silver bracelet with inlay of lapis lazuli, coral, and turquoise, 1999.

joined the U.S. Army and served from 1986–89. He attended Navajo Community College in Tsalie, Arizona, and later the University of New Mexico. After his service with the army, Haskie experimented on his own, cutting and soldering silver to make jewelry. In 1990 and 1991, he learned to do lapidary work. As he developed as an artist, he refined his work and used his imagination to derive creative designs.

Haskie initially draws a jewelry design before working with silver or gold. He tries to explore different avenues and ideas. For several years, Haskie's work has been recognizable not only for its intricate detail but also for his use of coral. Haskie refers to these as "inlay collages that are inspired by the sky, mountains, and the early sunrise." The designs in part reflect his surroundings at Lukachukai, Arizona. According to Haskie, "The Red Mesa sunsets and the Chuska mountains and cliffs are reflected in my work."[7] Haskie has won numerous awards for his jewelry, including the Best of Show award at the Heard Museum Guild Indian Fair & Market in 2000 for a silver concho belt with inlaid coral; Best of Classification in 2004; and Best of Show for another concho belt in 2007. Haskie's use of coral has distinguished his work.

Verma Nequatewa (Hopi, b. 1949) began an apprenticeship with her uncle Charles Loloma around 1966. Nequatewa has signed her distinctive work with the Hopi feminine word for beauty, *Sonwai*, since 1989. It complements her uncle's name, which was the masculine word with the same meaning. Nequatewa worked with her uncle for more than twenty years. In that time she not only learned specific jewelry-making techniques, but she also learned to distinguish quality stones and to develop a keen design sense. According to Nequatewa, "Charles taught that beauty is all around us on Hopi, in the environment, in the culture, in ceremony. His wisdom, his attitude, his artistic insights were wonderful. They are probably the greatest influence on what I do."[8]

Although she is accomplished at stone inlay, Nequatewa is equally accomplished at metalsmithing. She also has an expert ability to create color patterns, which she attributes to working with her uncle, although she has received much credit and recognition for her individual creations.

In 2005, Edison Cummings began to experiment with patterns in wood and stone for bracelets, pendants, and bolo ties. Cummings, who is best known for his ability to create raised metal forms, was already familiar with the properties of ironwood. Cummings had carved ironwood into handles and finials for teapots and had used ironwood with other silver items. Cummings began to carve and inset sections of ironwood along with fossilized ivory, turquoise, and coral. Although these appear to be Loloma inspired, Cummings' training first as a silversmith led him to embellish the stone and woodwork with inset bezel-set stones. This feature distinguishes his work from that of other jewelers.

A collaborative team who has created their own technique for stone patterning is that of Carl

Raymond Yazzie inlay bracelet, "Life's Beginning," of coral, lapis lazuli, turquoise, sugilite, opal, and 14k gold, 2004. This received a Best of Division award at the Heard Museum Guild Indian Fair & Market.

Verma Nequatewa (Sonwai) bracelets of turquoise, lapis lazuli, coral, silver, and 18k gold, 2005.

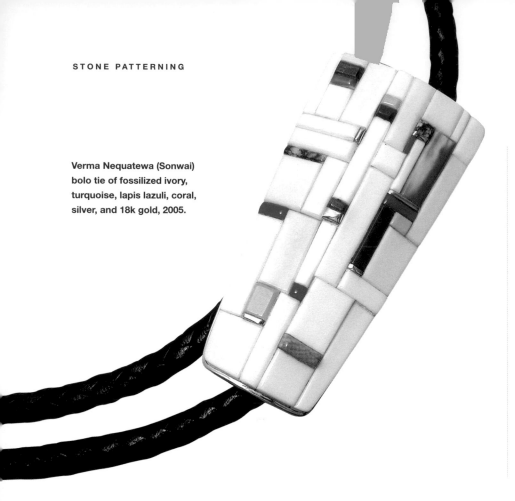

Verma Nequatewa (Sonwai) bolo tie of fossilized ivory, turquoise, lapis lazuli, coral, silver, and 18k gold, 2005.

and Irene Clark. Carl Clark (Navajo, b. 1952) was originally trained as a civil engineer and prefers to work on larger items such as the bracelets, bolos, and buckles. Irene Clark (Navajo, b. 1950) likes to design and make delicate jewelry such as earrings, rings, and pendants. Carl Clark learned to make silver jewelry in 1973 and made his first inlay ring in 1975. The silverwork is accomplished as the first step in their jewelry-making process.

A single bracelet made by the Clarks can incorporate as many as 5,000 to 6,000 stones. They developed a method of laminating layers of finely cut sheets of turquoise, sugilite, lapis lazuli, coral, jet, and other stones, which have been arranged into a patterned design. Then they crosscut the layered sheets into sections that are arranged into the various jewelry forms. Their work looks like an extremely fine mosaic, but instead of applying individual stones with an adhesive, the Clarks apply sections of the patterned designs they have created through the unique process they developed.

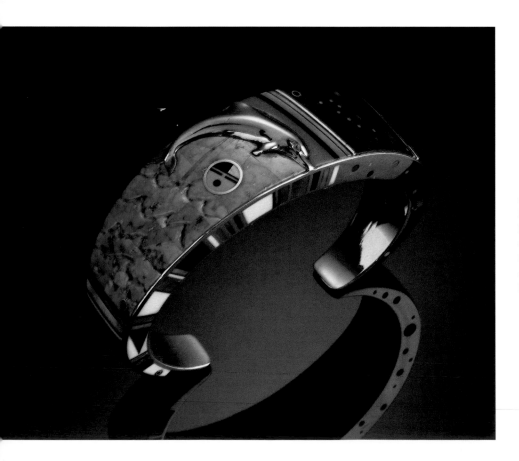

Jesse Monongya inlay bracelet of turquoise, lapis lazuli, coral, jet, opal, shell, and 14k gold, 1990s. Monongya appliquéd an eagle design on the bracelet interior.

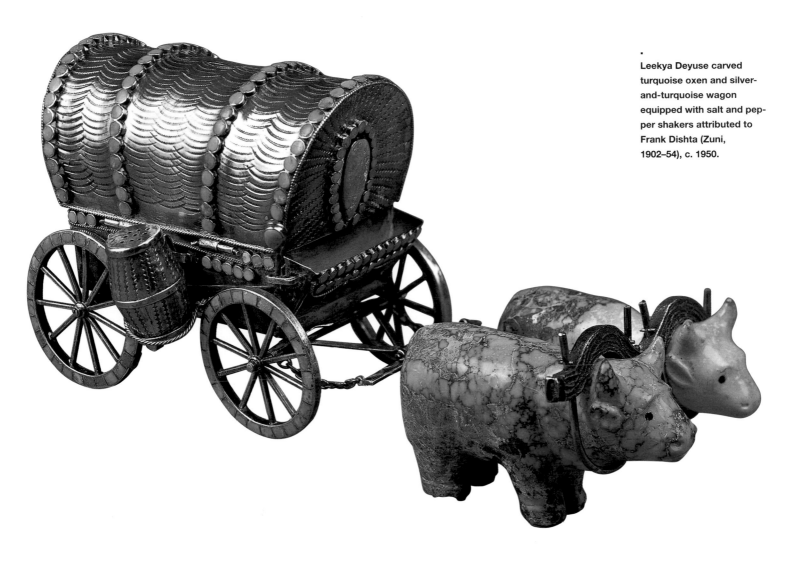

Leekya Deyuse carved turquoise oxen and silver-and-turquoise wagon equipped with salt and pepper shakers attributed to Frank Dishta (Zuni, 1902–54), c. 1950.

Carvings in Stone and Shell

Historically, stone carving for jewelry is associated with the jewelers of Zuni Pueblo. Leekya Deyuse, Teddy Weahkee, Leo Poblano, and other jewelers working in the 1930s were known for the three-dimensional forms they carved into small sculptures or smaller carvings they made into jewelry. A transformation had begun at Zuni Pueblo in the early 1900s when Zuni lapidarists began to carve and sell three-dimensional forms similar to those associated with ritual. The small animals have been termed fetishes by outsiders. Also, the term "fetish necklace" was coined from carved figures strung on necklaces.

At Zuni Pueblo, trader C. G. Wallace provided carvers with hand tools that included fine

files, grinding equipment, and, in some instances, studio space. He also was a source of turquoise for carvers and encouraged them to carve animal forms similar to those excavated at Hawikku Pueblo.

Perhaps the best-known carver is Leekya Deyuse (1889–1966). Leekya had been one of the laborers employed at Hawikku Pueblo.[9] His best-known carvings include bears carved from a local Zuni stone, a range of turquoise figures, and small sculptures with the bases carved of turquoise, coral, shell, or jet, as well as those without bases that were strung in necklaces. Leekya's animals frequently share anthropomorphic characteristics that distinguish them from the work of other carvers.

Edna Leki (Zuni, b. about 1930) creates bead necklaces and hand-carves pendants of birds and other animals that she includes in necklaces. Leki

Charles Loloma carved
turquoise corn maidens
with 14k gold, 1971.

Edna Leki necklace of
turquoise beads, carved
turquoise animals, and 14k
gold clasp, 1980s.

learned lapidary skills from her father, Teddy Weahkee, a well-known
Zuni jeweler who specialized in carving. Leki and family members have per-
petuated the carving tradition, each in their
own individual style. One of her daughters,
Dinah Gasper, creates fetish necklaces and at
times uses non-traditional materials such as fossilized ivory for carving. Another daughter, Lena
Boone, and a son, Anderson Weahkee, are known
for their carved three-dimensional figures made
from a variety of stones.

Charles Loloma brought attention to the technique of carving by creating the carved corn maidens in 1971. Always an innovator, Loloma's corn
maidens were primarily created in inlay patterns
much like his bracelets. At times he enhanced
wood and stones with minimalist carving and at
other times carved stones to achieve texture. In
1971, Loloma carved a double corn maiden of
turquoise with incised lines that look like the kernels of corn.

In the 1990s, Charles Supplee (Hopi/French,
b. 1959) began to take the concept of the corn
maiden a step further, creating stylized Hopi maidens in carved stone and fabricated or cast metal.
Supplee has also popularized a pendant shaped like
an ear of corn. The corn is carved to delineate the
kernels, and the husk is formed of fabricated metal.
Supplee has also used the lost wax technique to
fashion corn pendants and has inset stones and dia-

Near left: Charles Supplee carved coral pendant with fabricated 14k gold, and diamonds, 2003.

Below: Charles Supplee lost wax cast and textured 14k gold maiden with carved Tibetan turquoise features and diamonds, 1993.

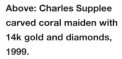

Above: Charles Supplee carved coral maiden with 14k gold and diamonds, 1999.

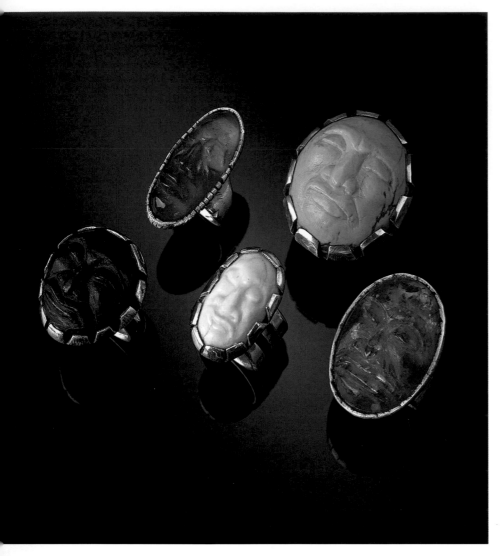

monds to further enhance the work.

Supplee learned basic jewelry techniques by watching his father work. By the age of twelve Supplee was familiar with some basic skills. After graduating from high school in Flagstaff, Supplee moved to Scottsdale, where he found work repairing jewelry for some of the Fifth Avenue shops. During this time he met French jeweler Pierre Touraine who had an interest in American Indian jewelry and in seeing contemporary work develop. Beginning around 1982, Touraine taught Supplee some additional skills that included diamond setting and lost wax casting but also encouraged him to draw upon his Hopi heritage for design inspiration. Touraine introduced Supplee to gallerist Lovena Ohl around 1985. Ohl, who was known for her interest in encouraging young American Indian artists, gave Supplee his first gallery show. Supplee continues to explore new avenues in his artwork, utilizing the diverse skills and techniques he has learned.

A few other artists carve stones occasionally, often to add texture or lines to the work. One jeweler who carves faces in various stones for the settings in the rings he makes is James Faks, who became interested in carving when he was fourteen. He began carving wood and then larger stone sculptures. Around 2002, he began carving small stones that he inset into silver rings. The carvings, usually of turquoise, amber, fossilized ivory, or jet, often share facial-feature characteristics of defined noses, lips, and eyes that have a Mayan look to them. Interestingly, Faks's mother is of Mayan heritage.

Above: James Faks fabricated silver rings with carved turquoise, fossilized ivory, and jet, 2002–04.

Left: Charles Supplee lost wax cast pendant of 14k gold with sugilite, turquoise, and diamonds, 2004.

Christina Eustace silver necklace
and ring with carved sugilite and
coral, coral earrings with 14k
gold appliqué, 2006.

Bead Necklaces

In the Southwest, stones such as turquoise and jet have been made into bead jewelry for centuries. Shells were traded from the coasts and cut and shaped into beads with stone tools. Later, coral was imported and fashioned into beads for necklaces as well. In the early 1900s, Zuni jewelers began to add carved figurative forms to necklaces.

With the use of better tools in the 1970s, jewelers Benny Aguilar and Charles Lovato (Santo Domingo, 1937–87) made very fine and delicate shell and stone beads. Lovato at times used melon shells and mussels that reflected the red, brown, or beige earth tones of the land, combining beads to create a blend colors. His necklaces were known for his incorporation of intricate beads arranged with color gradation. He would also insert individual turquoise or gold beads into necklaces. Lovato was also a respected painter and poet.

Lovato attended the Santa Fe Indian School, where he studied art with painter Jose Rey Toledo. He worked at Frank Patania's Thunderbird Shop from 1948 until Patania's death in 1968. Lovato credited Patania as being "a top master craftsman."[10] Lovato was honored, along with Charles Loloma, in the 1991 exhibit *Jewelry of the Southwest: Pueblo Tradition and Innovation* at the Wheelwright Museum in Santa Fe.

Some jewelers like Joe B. and Terry Reano (Santo Domingo, b. 1940 and 1935, respectively) prefer to use hand tools for cutting, grinding, and polishing beads. Working in the old style, they fashion necklaces of stones and shells just as their ancestors had. Both jewelers learned jewelry-making techniques from their parents. Terry Reano recalls helping her mother make thunderbird-style necklaces, which were popular in Santo Domingo during the Depression era. The couple has made a conscious decision to use the old style of bead making rather than use the electric tools that are almost exclusively employed by bead makers today.

Multi-strand coral bead
necklace, 1930s.

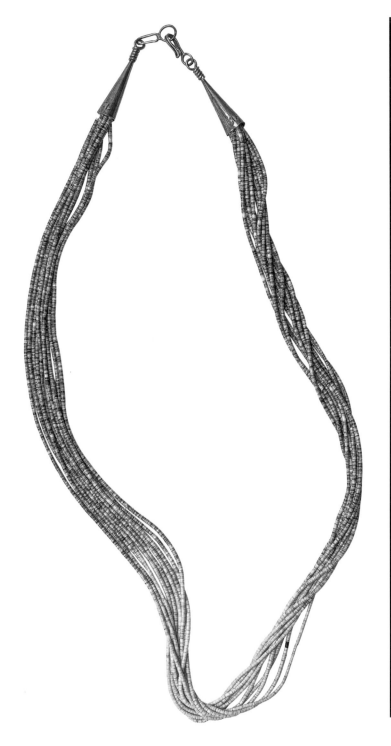

Charles Lovato shaded
necklace of white shell,
olivella shell, tortoise shell,
and 14k gold, 1970-80.

Joe B. and Terry Reano
Carico Lake turquoise
necklace with silver, 1996.

Cheryl Yestewa opal, sug-
ilite, and 14k gold bead
necklace, 2000.

Yazzie Johnson and Gail
Bird turquoise and lapis
lazuli necklace with clasps
of azurite, 1980s.

**Yazzie Johnson and Gail
Bird nine-strand freshwater
pearls and peridot necklace
with Yowah opal clasps and
18k gold, 2000.**

Yazzie Johnson and Gail Bird "Flying Things" necklace, five strands of onyx, hematite, and howlite beads with snowflake obsidian clasps and pendant of Mexican agate, psilomelane, and silver, 1988.

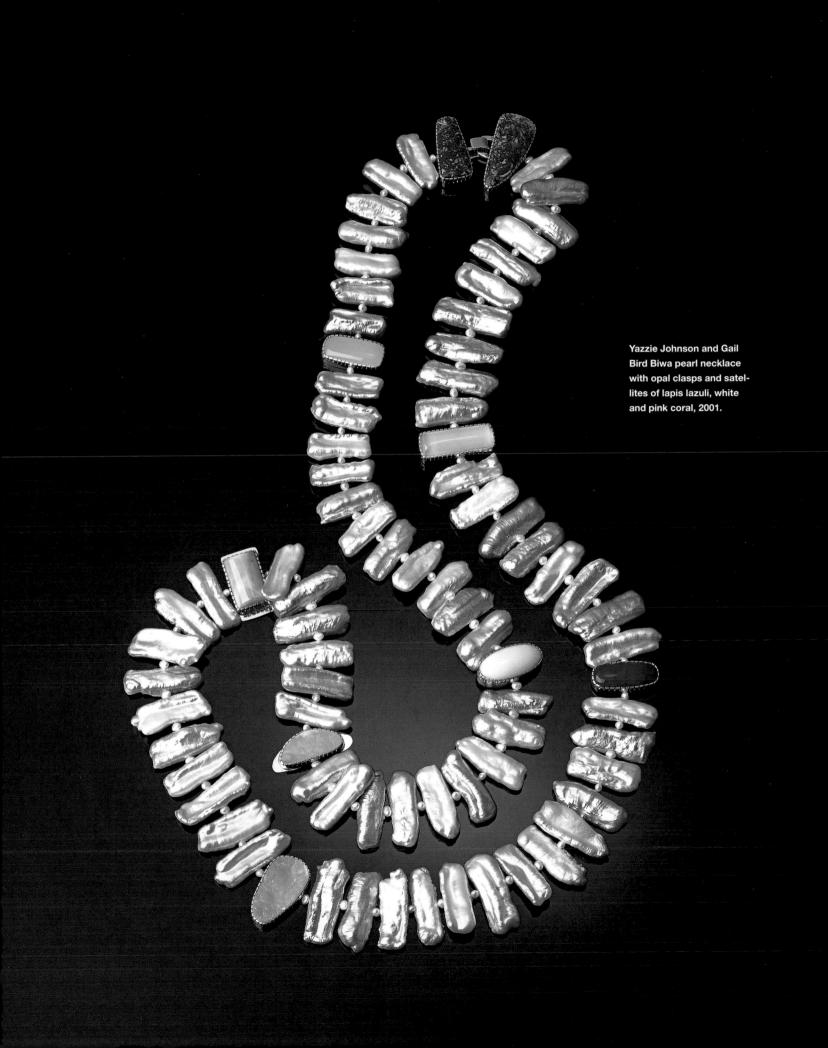

Yazzie Johnson and Gail
Bird Biwa pearl necklace
with opal clasps and satellites of lapis lazuli, white
and pink coral, 2001.

Navajo/Hopi jeweler Cheryl Yestewa (Hopi/Navajo, b. 1958) was born in Keams Canyon, Arizona. Her father, Carroll Yestewa, carved katsina dolls and did some silversmithing. Cheryl admits to having an "interest in pretty rocks" as a child.[11] She is a self-taught jeweler who began working with silver and gemstones as a young adult. Now she specializes in lapidary work and goldsmithing and prefers creating beads of natural turquoise and other gemstones.

Yazzie Johnson and Gail Bird made their first necklace in 1980. It was based on a South American glass trade bead milagro necklace that had small milagros, or amulets, attached. They initially cleaned old glass beads and strung multiple strands with small stone-set pendants or satellites. By the early 1980s, they began experimenting with other stones, coral, and pearls. Their necklaces began to be distinguished by stone-set clasps, which were designed to be worn at the side rather than the back of the neck. They began to use a wide variety of pearls selected for quality and luster.

Victor Beck (Navajo, b. 1941) combines turquoise and coral to create necklaces that are inspired by traditional jewelry yet are a departure toward more contemporary work. Beck became interested in making jewelry while a student at Northern Arizona University in Flagstaff. He began in the ceramics program, but the required nine hours of jewelry class work eventually changed his life's path. Beck found that jewelry making was a perfect match for him. He continued his studies at State University of New York in New Paltz, where he further developed his concepts about jewelry design. Beck also drew inspiration from Charles Loloma's inlay work and continues to incorporate some of those ideas into his work.

Victor Beck necklace of turquoise, coral, jet, shell, and 14k gold, 2000.

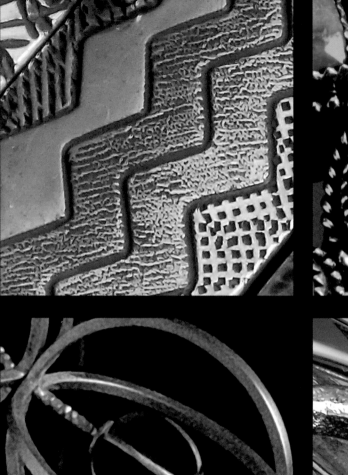

EMERGING ARTISTS

Contemporary Jewelry Today

Contemporary American Indian jewelry has continued to experience change and growth. At times, contemporary jewelry shares a connection with historic works, either through materials or techniques used. At other times contemporary works do not have a direct connection with jewelry from the past.

Today's young artists, ages twenty to thirty, may share experiences that emphasize community and family like those of the generations before them. Some also have unique experiences that include formal training in art or design at competitive universities and select art schools. This new generation has benefited from the innovations of Charles Loloma, but they were not directly influenced like the generation before them who saw Loloma's designs unfold in a dramatic, influential, and, at times, a very direct and intimate way. This new generation has not experienced the same barriers to creating nontraditional jewelry. Although there are still those who would limit American Indian artists to "traditional" materials and techniques, there are many others who accept the avant garde work this new generation creates.

Generalities can never be made for a generation of artists. Some young jewelers working today grew up in homes where making jewelry was enmeshed in life, commerce, and community. Others did not. Some young jewelers learned by observing their parents make jewelry and receiving encouragement from them. Others had parents who did not make jewelry. Instead these young jewelers learned by experimenting or observing a friend who was generous enough to illustrate a particular technique or skill. Some jewelers in this younger generation took jewelry classes in high school and then design and art classes in college. Some never planned to make a career of jewelry but found that they could adapt their art interests to the media and they are quite accomplished at creating and executing jewelry designs.

The baby boomer–generation of jewelers—those born from 1945 to 1957—have been referred to as the post–World War II experimentally inclined generation.[1] The diverse range of jewelry made by those of the boomer generation, the adoption of gold rather than silver, the use of stones other than turquoise, and the creation of new designs and techniques seems to substantiate this hypothesis.

Like the young generation of jewelers today, the baby boomer jewelers learned their techniques in a variety of ways that included experimentation, learning through reading the 1944 book *Navajo and Pueblo Silversmiths in the Southwest* by John Adair, and, for some, learning directly from a family member. Many from the baby boomer generation had grandparents who lived in the agrarian Southwest, where farming or raising sheep or cattle was an important aspect of daily life. For some, that lifestyle was supplemented by making and selling Native American art forms such as jewelry, pottery, and weaving—items that were once made for personal use.

Some parents of baby boomers went to boarding schools in larger cities, and after completing high school, with the shifting economy of the day, sought mainstream jobs to support their families. For those families, the process of a family member directly teaching another family member an art form was reduced or did not occur. Many jewelers from the baby boomer generation attended universities where they studied art. The difference between jewelers of their generation and jewelers of today's young generation is that those of the young generation began working with fewer restrictions on their work. Consequently, they had more freedom to explore. But the question still remains whether a large collector base will readily accept nontraditional, contemporary work.

Keri Ataumbi

Keri Ataumbi (Kiowa, b. 1971) comes from a family that respects and honors art. She is a painter, a landscape designer, a jeweler, and a jewelry-making instructor. Ataumbi has worked to learn diverse jewelry techniques, and she incorporates unusual designs in her metalwork. Of the diverse art forms in which she works, Ataumbi notes that learning to make jewelry was the most complex because of the many different techniques involved.

Ataumbi was born in Wyoming and grew up on the Wind River Reservation where her mother, Jeri Ah-Be-Hill, had a trading post that held cases of beadwork and silverwork. As a child of nine years old, Ataumbi remembers the personal impact of initially seeing jewelry by Charles Loloma. One of his bracelets gave her a deep and lasting appreci-

Opposite: Keri Ataumbi necklace "Tahlee's Parents" of silver, 14k gold, and peridot, 2005.

Right: Keri Ataumbi ring of silver, 14k gold, and amber, 2006.

ation of jewelry. Ataumbi identifies several influences on her artwork that stem from her childhood. One influence—the hide paintings that she saw in her mother's trading post—made an indelible impression on the paintings she creates. But her jewelry was directly influenced by visits to the foundry where her father's bronze sculptures were cast, as well as time spent in his studio. Other family experiences and personal adornment have also influenced Ataumbi. She and her sister had their ears pierced while still infants, and the sisters were always bedecked in jewelry.

The two sisters pursued their individual interests in art. Ataumbi's sister, Teri Greeves, is well known for her unconventional and contemporary beading of sneakers, umbrellas, leather-covered trunks, and other items. Ataumbi busily pursues her creative talents in various fields. Ten years ago she began doing landscape maintenance and installation, and eventually she began to design landscapes as well. She started designing gardens for private clients and now designs for a New Mexico developer and helps new homeowners plan their landscapes.

Ataumbi attributes her work in metal to her interest in art and her childhood experiences. Since no one in the family made jewelry, Ataumbi was forced to learn about it in other ways. She studied jewelry-making techniques at Santa Fe Community College, where she initially learned casting techniques. Also, in 2000, she traveled to Bali to study the jewelry-making techniques from indigenous artists of that country. While there, she apprenticed with local artist Nyoman Partha, who helped her

refine her fabrication skills. Ataumbi incorporated many of the techniques she learned in a necklace she made for the 47th Annual Heard Museum Guild Indian Fair & Market in 2005 that references a Kiowa story called "Tahlee's Parents." Sections of the necklace were cast to look like small oak branches through a method similar to lost wax casting. Ataumbi added small peridot to resemble acorns.

Ataumbi also studied enameling at the Penland School of Craft in North Carolina in 2005. Enam-

eling enables her to achieve colored metalworks and accomplish elements of design that would otherwise be impossible. Much of her jewelry relates to themes of nature and some directly resemble plants or animals, while others incorporate those designs in an abstract form. She made one necklace with green enameled floral shapes that contained metal forms radiating from each center that look like floral stamen. Other jewelry forms look like delicate leaf patterns executed in gold and accented with

diamonds. For the 2006 Heard Museum Guild Indian Fair & Market, Ataumbi made a silver ring with a design of a bee appliquéd to the hinged top. When open, the ring reveals amber placed over a plate of gold with pierce-work circles that look like a honeycomb.

Although she incorporates stones and freshwater pearls in her jewelry, Ataumbi emphasizes the metalwork. At times, she selects pearls for their natural but unusual shapes, such as the time she selected a pearl that looked like the eyes of a frog. She next cast a frog in silver and then added the pearl for its eyes. These and other animal forms were shaped into jewelry for a 2006 sales show of her work called "The Birds and the Bees," held at the shop at the Institute of American Indian Art in Santa Fe. Keeping with this theme, Ataumbi made a silver necklace with a front opening that has a decorative element of a butterfly on one side and a flower on the other. The two design elements are suspended, giving the illusion that the butterfly is nearing but perhaps never quite reaching the flower.

At times, Ataumbi concentrates solely on the metalwork, allowing it to convey the artistic concept. One example is a bracelet based on the elements of water, the prototype of which was made for the 2006 Indian Market in Santa Fe. Although the silver bracelet is an openwork cube rather than a conventional circle, the small openwork circles of silver and 18k gold appliquéd to the cube convey the sense of water droplets. The different sizes of the circles capture the essence of water.

Ataumbi attributes teaching others the processes of jewelry making as the catalyst that has helped refine her skills. She has taught at the University of New Mexico campuses in Los Alamos and Albuquerque and at the Institute of American Indian Art in Santa Fe.

Like other jewelers of her generation, Ataumbi is interested in creating jewelry with articulated properties. She created a necklace for the 2006 Heard Fair that consists of openwork silver wire that surrounds smaller segmented silver beads she made and oxidized to a darker color to contrast with the silver wire. They give an organic sense to the necklace. Also, strung on the necklace are small, fine silver beads that add a sense of lightness.

The faceted beads have the capability of spinning on the necklace.

When speaking of her work, Ataumbi indicates that there are many forms of jewelry. "There are standard mass-produced pieces, staid mass marketable pieces, the fashion market aimed to support trendy baubles and ethnic jewelry rooted in tradition that more and more is being made in mass for tourists. Emerging across the world and standing apart from those approaches to jewelry is the unique category of wearable art. In creating this type of jewelry the artist develops a concept and design, addresses the relationship between object and the body and, thus, engages in and deepens the discussion of fine art. My jewelry has a conceptual narrative exploration at its core. I use traditional Kiowa imagery and materials in a contemporary form and nature as inspiration to create a small sculpture complete upon its own as well as jewelry worn on the body."[2]

Keri Ataumbi necklace of silver and silver faceted beads, 2006.

Jared Chavez

Silversmith Jared Chavez (San Felipe, b. 1982) learned jewelry-making techniques from his father but also graduated from Georgetown University with a bachelor of fine arts degree in 2005. Chavez is known for his unusually shaped silver containers with abstract designs that often reflect cities and houses or quiet pastoral scenes of New Mexico.

Chavez grew up in a household where jewelry was a way of life. His father, Richard, excelled in making jewelry with complex abstract stone inlay accented by elegant silver or gold metalwork. Although Jared Chavez had an interest in art, he had only a peripheral interest in jewelry, preferring digital art to silverwork. During his senior year of high school, Chavez made plans to study art in Fort Collins, Colorado, at Colorado State University. That same year, Chavez visited his sister, Cynthia, in Washington, D.C., where she worked at the National Museum of the American Indian. During the trip, they visited Georgetown University. Cynthia Chavez suggested that her brother consider applying to the university. Once back home in New Mexico, Chavez decided to apply, although his plans for college were firm and he and a friend had already agreed to be roommates at Colorado State.

To his surprise, he was accepted to the university and had to choose between his plans to go to Colorado and an opportunity to live in one of the most vibrant cities in the U.S. Chavez chose Georgetown and made plans to attend the following year and study art.

As time grew closer to begin his class work at Georgetown, Chavez worried that the small art department would not meet his interests. Once he began classes, he found a small but stimulating environment that encouraged exploration and creativity. One of his professors in particular, print instructor Calvin Custen, challenged Chavez and allowed him to work with a range of techniques. Although Chavez's primary interest was in digital art, he soon became enthralled with different aspects of printmaking and explored woodblock printing, intaglio, and chinkole.

Chavez was working in silver before attending Georgetown and first participated in Indian Market in Santa Fe in 1995. Chavez continued to work in silver and participate in Indian Market with the exception of his freshman year at Georgetown. He began to see a connection between the printing processes and silverwork. Each served as a palette for the abstract designs he would create.

Chavez distinguished his silverwork from that of other jewelers', including his father's, and related

Jared Chavez silver platter, "The Chaos of Creation," 2005.

graphic look acquired in printmaking and applies those concepts to metalwork.

In 2002, Chavez made his first silver container fitted with a lid. Called "Four Elements," it is divided into four panels, each containing designs of elements of the natural world—earth, wind, fire, and water. For the 2003 Indian Market in Santa Fe, Chavez made his first large-scale container. Called "Two Worlds Under One Sky," the silver, lidded container had three main design fields: one on the elongated and curved side, one on the shorter, straight side, and a final one on the top. On the longer side is an abstract depiction of home at San Felipe with a tree-lined drive, while on the shorter side are clusters of buildings reaching for the sky at home and at school in Washington, D.C. According to Chavez, "This piece was created to reflect the dichotomy of lifestyles I was living between my home in San Felipe Pueblo and my life at Georgetown."[4]

In 2004, Chavez made a large-scale silver platter entitled "The Chaos of Creation." He carved wooden forms to the desired shape and was ready to place the sheet of silver between them to form the shape. Since he did not have a hydraulic press, he needed something with tremendous weight to get the silver to conform to the shape of the wooden male and female forms. His father jacked up his truck, and they placed the wooden mold outfitted with the silver plate under one of the tires. The weight of the truck pressed the plate to the desired form. Chavez was now ready to enhance the plate with the abstract design he had selected. He also created and enhanced a silver base with stamp work. According to Chavez, "The overall design of this piece reflected the general havoc and chaos of the creation of the universe. All life, illustrated through stamp work, could be seen to expand from one central point in the center of the platter outward and continue onto the base as well."[5]

At Santa Fe Market in 2005, Chavez created another large container with an unusual shape, entitled "Commemoration." Purchased by the Smithsonian's National Museum of the American Indian, the curved shape of the box is similar to the shape of the new museum building in Washington, D.C. According to Chavez, "I had started working on

it to the prints and the digital composite photography he was making. The prints were abstract and, at times, depicted buildings, combining shots of different buildings to give the appearance of being one building. According to Chavez, "My designs are not specific to one thing. I apply them to everything I do."[3]

Although the viewer can see a notable connection to the print designs and the silverwork designs, Chavez is aware of the way the processes of making these varied art forms is also connected. One printmaking process, etching, involves creating a design in metal by adding acid to the surface. Woodblock printmaking also involves altering the surface of a material. When silver or another metal is stamped to make a design, the surface of the silver is also altered. To Chavez, all of these processes share similarities. He knows in advance how the process will change the surface and how the resulting texture will affect the design. Chavez takes the

the idea for the shape of the piece for the 2004 Indian Market, but had no idea what narrative to use for the walls. With time running out fast, the shape for the vessel was shelved until the following year. This happened to be my last year at Georgetown, during which it was possible to complete a series of four 2 x 6-inch carved wooden panels, each of which depicted a year at the University. The scenes represented involved emotional states, influential people in my life, and an overall outline of what shaped my life up until the point of graduation. With these panels, I was able to finalize the design for 'Commemoration,' tying in the meaning of the vessel to both the completion of the Smithsonian's Museum of the American Indian, which I had seen from start to finish, as well as my own journey through four years at GU."[6]

Chavez plans his containers and their designs by first drawing them on a large sketchpad. For the unusual-shaped containers, it is also necessary to figure out the dimensions in order to accomplish the desired form. Chavez's designs curve and have a sense of movement. Building walls are not straight, but expand abstractly. In order to trans-

form these curved lines of his drawings to stamped lines of silver, Chavez takes sections of guitar wire and places them in the desired curved shapes on the silver. He lightly tapes them in place and strikes them with a hammer to make the stamped impressions in the silver. After making the primary outlines this way, Chavez textures areas of the silver with stamp work.

From January through March 2006, Chavez attended a three-month intensive program at the Revere Academy in San Francisco. There, he took twenty-two classes, which ranged from the fundamentals of jewelry fabrication to more advanced techniques in stone setting, casting, and forging. The knowledge he gained was a valuable resource that he is implementing in his current jewelry. According to Chavez, "The structured training of these techniques allowed me to see all the directions I could go in my work."[7]

In 2006, collector Norman Sandfield commissioned Chavez to make a silver seed jar. He made the jar the requested three-inch diameter and also completed a six-inch diameter jar for the Indian Market at Santa Fe that same year. According to

Jared Chavez silver bracelet, with designs made by hammering guitar string on a silver surface and by stamp work, 2000.

Chavez, "Having never made a seed jar, it took some time to think of the design. Eventually, I went with the concept of the creation of plant life. The designs on the pot reflect the turmoil and struggle of seeds to become and basically exist as fully grown plants. I also used the title as a play on meanings for both the germination of seeds and the germination of this very piece to come into existence."[8] For the same market, Chavez made a series of works that all centered around the concept of the play of light and color off metal. The centerpiece of this idea came in the form of a concho belt with an abstract design entitled, "Dancing in the Moonlight." This piece used confined areas of highly polished silver on top of a gunmetal gray patina to create a dance of reflected color and light while worn.

After concentrating on making silverwork for an intensive period of time, often for the Indian Market in Santa Fe, the Heard Fair, and other events, Chavez likes to return to his studio in San Felipe that houses his canvases and print-making materials. Chavez finds it almost necessary for him to practice other art forms to keep his designs fresh and his mind in a constant state of creation.

Jared Chavez silver seed jar, 2006.

Jared Chavez "Dancing in the
Moonlight," silver belt, 2006.

**Jared Chavez, "City Scape,"
intaglio and chinkole, 2005.**

David Gaussoin

David Gaussoin (Picuris/Navajo/French, b. 1975) learned to make jewelry from his mother, Connie, who has a photograph of David at age five or six watching her solder metal. Her studio was in a corner of the den, a converted garage, and Gaussoin remembers watching Saturday morning cartoons while his mother made jewelry. His mother encouraged him to make jewelry, and when he was about eight or nine years old, he began making rings out of half-round wire. Gaussoin learned basic skills such as soldering, buffing, and cleaning the jewelry and later learned how to make a bezel for a simple stone. His first major piece was a hatband—a half-domed piece with copper loops on the back. He learned other skills such as tufa casting, hand stamping, and inlay either by direct instruction or through observation. When he was in high school, his mother was taking classes at the Institute of American Indian Arts (IAIA). David learned the technique of cuttlefish bone casting when he was allowed to watch the class at the college.

After high school, Gaussoin initially attended the University of New Mexico in Albuquerque and then transferred to IAIA, where he took a two-dimensional art class from Linda Lomahaftewa and a portfolio and business of art class with Karita Coffey. He returned to UNM and completed a bachelor of business administration degree in business marketing in 1999.

At UNM, Gaussoin took a small-scale sculpture class from instructor Connie DeYoung, an artist who creates large-scale sculpture. He was the only jeweler in the class but still found the techniques useful. One of the processes he learned was lost wax casting. While in college, Gaussoin would return home on the weekends and work on jewelry.

After graduation, he spent three months in Europe where he developed an appreciation for Scandinavian designs including glasswork as well as jewelry. In Germany he appreciated the incorporation of steel in jewelry, an influence that is apparent in his current work. In a necklace made in 2006, Gaussoin provided flexibility to the construction through the use of stainless steel rivets that connect sections of the necklace. He taught himself how to use rivets in jewelry by trial and error after reading a book with information on the topic.

David Gaussoin tufa-cast silver bracelet, 2006.

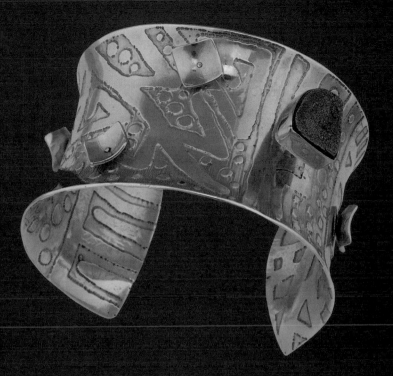

David Gaussoin bracelet of silver, 14k gold, and drusy pyrite, 2006.

David Gaussoin necklace of silver, steel, and moonstone, 2006.

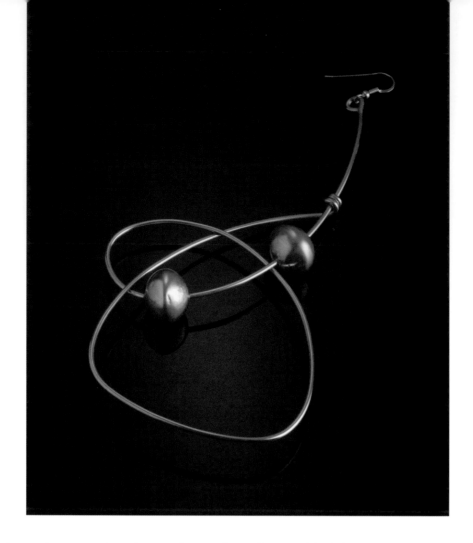

David Gaussoin silver
earring, 2005.

In 2005, Gaussion also used rivets in a bracelet. For that item, the rivets held in place small 14k gold plates. The rivets allow the small plates to move into different positions. The plates are abstract interpretations of flowers on Pueblo men's headdresses. To further enhance the bracelet, Gaussoin added acid-etched designs, both on the exterior and the interior of the bracelet. To accomplish this, he painted the silver with a mordant, leaving areas exposed on which to create the design. The silver is placed in the acid, and the etched pattern results. As in other jewelry techniques, timing is everything. If left too long, the silver will become paper-thin. When successfully completed, the colors in the Russian drusy complement the gold plates scattered on the surface.

Gaussoin is among a small number of American Indian artists who are drawn to fashion in addition to other art forms. The first fashion show in which Gaussoin included his work was held in conjunction with the Pueblo Opera Program in 2001. Some of his contemporaries were Dylan Poblano, Cochiti ceramist Virgil Ortiz, and clothing designer Patricia Michaels. The models for Gaussoin's jewelry wore black dresses. For the next two shows in 2002 and 2003, the models were draped in material that, according to Gaussoin, "served as a palette for the jewelry." Then, in 2004, Gaussoin decided to take a sewing class and began to design his clothing for the fashion show. In 2005 and 2006, the fashion shows were held during the week prior to Indian Market in Santa Fe and featured work by other young American Indian artists. Gaussoin's younger sister, Tazbah, modeled the fashions and jewelry in recent years. Gaussoin took classes at Duane Maktima's Pueblo V Institute, where he learned to make collar necklaces. In 2002, he taught classes at the Poeh Art Center in Tesuque. He has also demonstrated tufa-casting at the Heard Museum and taught business arts management and portfolio at IAIA.

David Gaussoin tufa-cast
and fabricated silver bracelet
with 14k gold, diamonds, and
drusy pyrite, 2006.

Wayne Nez Gaussoin

Wayne Nez Gaussoin (Picuris/Navajo/French, b. 1982) learned to make jewelry by watching his mother, Connie, and brother, David. Gaussoin began experimenting with jewelry when he was nine years old. He would go into his mother's studio, which at the time was inside their home in a corner of a room that held a pool table. As the jewelry making became more involved, the pool table became a workbench. Then, as they needed more room, the family took the pool table apart, transforming the former den into a studio. Today, the family garage has been converted into a studio shared by Wayne, his brother, and his mother. At times, his aunt, who makes micaceous pottery, also works in the studio.

Gaussoin began to enter his jewelry in youth competitions while he was in junior high school. He won awards at Indian Market in Santa Fe and at the Museum of Man in San Diego. He took drafting rather than art classes in high school and developed an interest in photography through journalism. He worked for the high school paper, and when they needed a photographer, he agreed to undertake the task. He got some basic instructions from his mother, and with the use of his Pentax K1000 35mm camera, developed skills that would later become an artistic interest.

After Gaussoin graduated from St. Michael's High School, he went to Santa Fe Community College, where he took business classes. He next studied at the University of New Mexico and then completed an associate of fine arts degree. He also took classes at the Institute of American Indian Arts, where he focused on photography. In 2005, he began attending the School of the Art Institute of Chicago, where he wanted to study jewelry and photography based on his experience and his portfolio. While there, Gaussoin took art classes including fashion design, art history, and computer modeling. He also took drawing and sculpture classes to strengthen his skills in those areas. He was particularly drawn to sculpture because of the parallels between sculpture and jewelry construction. Gaussoin found the open attitude of the Art Institute staff a direct contrast to the pervasive attitude in the southwest that silver and turquoise jewelry should remain traditional. By contrast, Gaussoin found that he could experiment with unlimited materials—anything from cooked noodles to balloons—in his sculpture classes.

Gaussoin likes to apply the same sense of freedom he used in sculpture classes to his jewelry creations. Although he works mainly with silver and gold, at times he adds exotic stones. This freedom to explore is evident in silver wire earrings he created in 2005. Currently, he is working to expand his skills in silver and is experimenting with textures and patinas. With the techniques that he has learned, he works to incorporate his own ideas through a minimalist style.

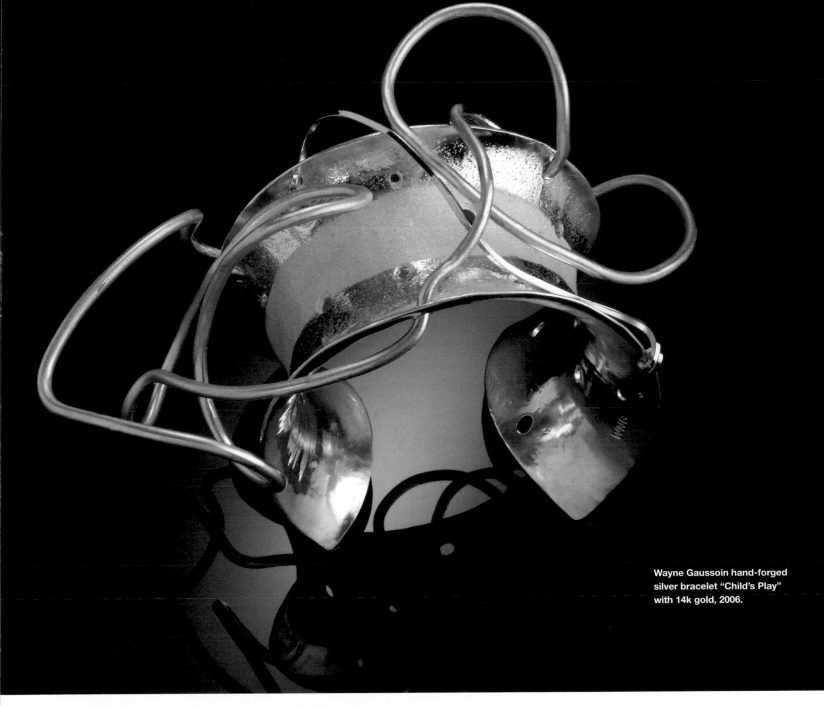

Wayne Gaussoin hand-forged
silver bracelet "Child's Play"
with 14k gold, 2006.

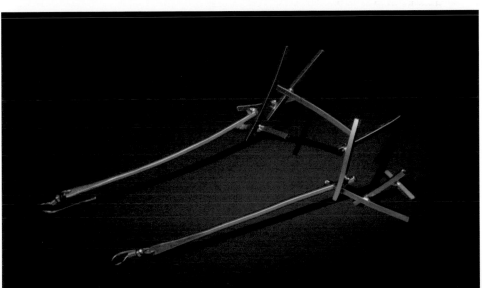

Wayne Gaussoin silver earrings, 2005.

Below: Wayne Gaussoin
"Picasso Face," tufa-cast
silver ring with drusy
quartzite and 14k gold,
2005.

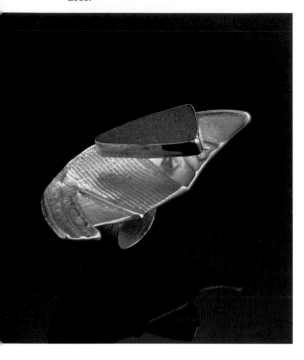

Right: Wayne Gaussoin
"Aver," silver necklace,
2006.

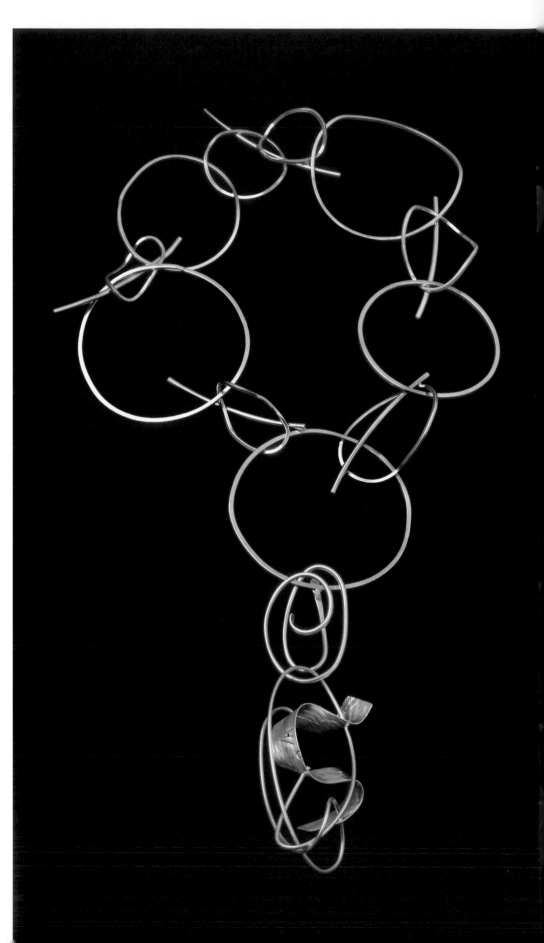

Dylan Poblano

ylan Poblano (Zuni, b. 1974) is a third-generation jeweler whose grandfather, Leo, was known for multistone inlay and whose mother, Veronica, developed a series of Disney character rings as a young jeweler. Poblano grew up playing in his mother's studio and learned by watching her create jewelry. When he was about eight years old, Poblano began experimenting in making jewelry, using small stones and scraps of silver left from the jewelry his mother made. At school in Zuni in the third grade, Poblano had jewelry craft instruction by Terry Gchachu. Around the age of twelve or thirteen he became more interested in making jewelry. After junior high Poblano was even more serious about art and began to enter jewelry and paintings in student art shows, including the one held at the Heard Museum.

While attending Albuquerque High School, Poblano sold his jewelry at an art fair in Hunter, New York. He began to think about art schools and was encouraged by a family friend and staff member of the Fashion Institute of Technology (FIT) in New York to attend FIT. Poblano also had some friends who were attending, and FIT seemed to suit his interests. After graduation, Poblano moved to New York to begin his studies at FIT. The curriculum included jewelry classes but also drawing, painting, and fashion design classes. Living in New York was quite a change of pace from life in Zuni, New Mexico. The two years that he spent at FIT broadened his horizons and al-

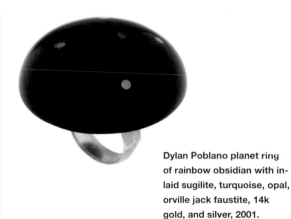

Dylan Poblano planet ring of rainbow obsidian with inlaid sugilite, turquoise, opal, orville jack faustite, 14k gold, and silver, 2001.

lowed Poblano to learn new techniques, including lost wax casting.

Poblano returned to Zuni, New Mexico, where he continued to experiment with jewelry design and fabrication. Poblano's emphasis is on inlay as well as metalwork, and he incorporates unusual stones as well as contemporary materials into his work. He has created several distinctive styles, including a series of works that center upon the solar system and the planets. They include a planet ring made of rainbow obsidian polished so that a ring of light reflects in the translucent stone, and several small spots of color are accomplished by inlaying diverse stones into the obsidian. He also made necklaces that represent the solar system. A September moon necklace was designed so that the planets encircled the wearer's neck. Another necklace in crystal and silver represented the lunar eclipse.

Left: Dylan Poblano silver, shell, and crystal ring, 2006.

Near right: Dylan Poblano silver ring with etched and oxidized design, 2001.

Above: Dylan Poblano silver dremel-textured and overlay bracelet, 2001.

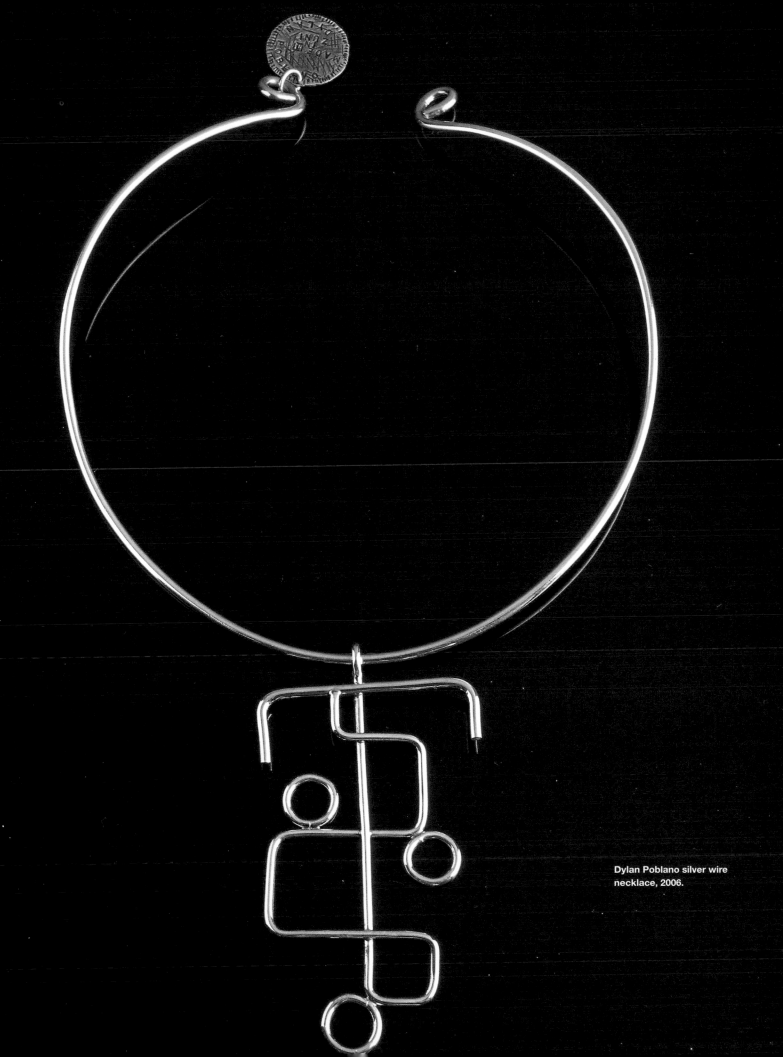

Dylan Poblano silver wire
necklace, 2006.

Poblano sketched and drew frequently during high school; one subject of his drawings was young women. He applied the concept to several of his metalworks, including an etched ring that contains a different woman's profile on each side. Poblano further enhanced the details of the etched silver surface by adding three types of oxidizer to the surface. When experimenting with pieces, he might add an accent of a face to metalwork or sketches of women to a bracelet. In 2001, Poblano created a bracelet using two different techniques; he did the design in silver overlay and then textured the background with the painstaking process of using a dremel tool to create small depressions in the silver.

Poblano has also made small half- to one-inch silver cast shoes based on different designer shoe styles and formed them as earrings or as charms for a bracelet. He has created a range of innovative designs in metal and semiprecious stones.

Dylan Poblano earrings of fluorite and silver, 2000.

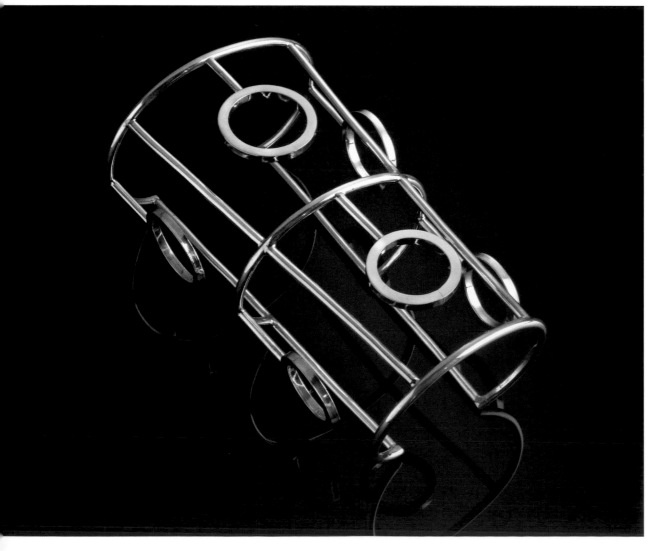

Dylan Poblano silver wire bracelet, 2006.

Maria Samora

Maria Samora silver, 14k gold, and diamond "Lattice Ring," 2006.

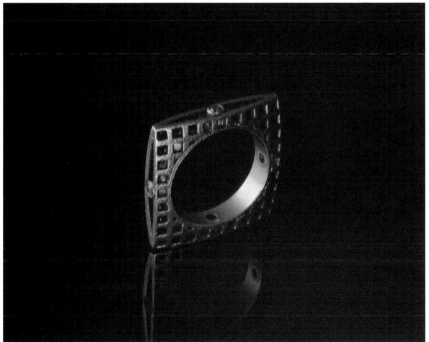

Maria Samora (Taos, b. 1975) grew up in Taos, New Mexico. Although her father, Frank, has told her that he made jewelry as a younger man, while growing up Samora observed her mother, Chien Motto, making jewelry. As a teenager, Samora also made some jewelry, usually out of beads. With the assistance of a scholarship, in 1993 she attended Pitzer College in Los Angeles for two and a half years. While there, Samora studied art, was particularly interested in photography, and also studied Spanish.

Samora took a break from school to travel in South America with the intent to explore photography and improve her Spanish. After the trip, in 1997, Samora returned home to Taos. She and a friend decided to take a jewelry class taught by Phil Poirier through the Taos branch of the University of New Mexico, for which Samora received a Taos Institute of Art scholarship. Samora quickly picked up the techniques of soldering, filing, and other basic skills. She approached Poirier about working with him as an apprentice after completing only two days of the class. Initially he declined, but within a few months an opening became available and he agreed to the working arrangement. Samora worked with Poirier side by side in his studio, but of equal importance was access to his extensive library and Poirier's encouragement of Samora to take a few hours daily to look at books, get ideas, and sketch designs. Samora found this opportunity to be rewarding, although she was more inclined to work directly with the metal to create designs rather than to sketch them in advance. She apprenticed with Poirier for five years, and Poirier continues to serve as Samora's mentor.

In 1998, Samora began to make her own jewelry. Initially, she worked in silver and then combined silver with gold because she likes the two tones and the contrasts of the two metals. Increasingly, but not exclusively, she works with 18k gold. She prefers the luster of 24k gold and the durability of 18k. To acquire the 24k look, she uses an Incan technique that adds a 24k gold finish to the metal. For some jewelry she creates, Samora will use a variety of patinas to add contrast and dimension.

For a bracelet and earring set made in 2006, she used geometric forms that appear simple at a glance, but when worn the intertwined geometric shapes combined with the patina provide a sculptural effect. The similar patina on the necklace also provides contrast for the work. Samora is drawn to properties of jewelry and has stated, "I like the way a design lays on the body—how it looks and how it makes you feel. The purpose of my art is to accentuate the body and capture the movement of the human form."[9]

In addition to her designs that are based on the interplay of geometric forms, Samora draws inspiration from nature for her jewelry. Some of her designs, such as a bracelet she created in 18k gold with hand-selected diamonds, are directly inspired by lily pads. For this bracelet and some of her other jewelry, Samora alloys her own 18k gold from pure 24k gold nuggets. She heats the nuggets in a crucible to a molten stage and then pours the molten metal to form an ingot. She then hammers the gold ingot and forms a sheet of metal from which she creates the lily pad shapes used in her jewelry. The diamonds are hammer-set with thick-gauge bezels.

Her studies of jewelry and art have also provided Samora a passion for Renaissance, Byzantine, and ancient styles, including Incan jewelry. Samora does not sketch her designs on paper, but instead approaches the materials directly by hand, manipulating the metals and stones and adding patinas and textures. Her studies of jewelry and life in Taos combine to capture the interplay of formality and informality that results in classic works with clean lines. According to Samora, "Growing up in Taos has provided me with a cultural and creative richness. Life in Taos is simple and beautiful, and I believe that my jewelry is a personal expression of this simplicity."[10]

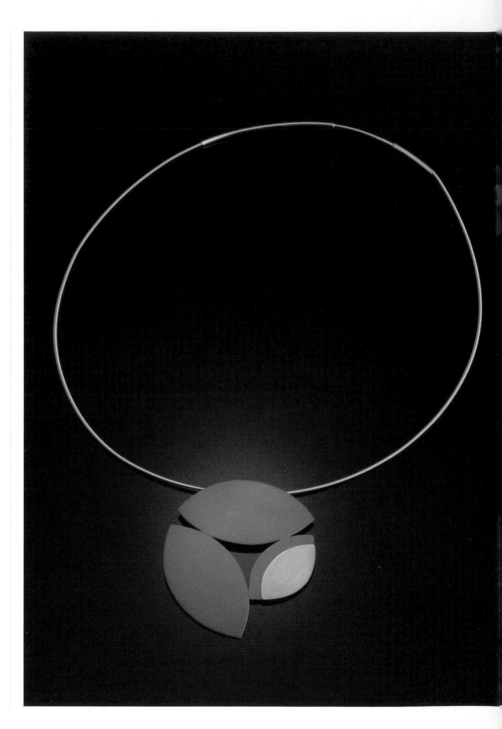

Maria Samora silver necklace, 2006.

Maria Samora silver bracelet, 2006.

Cody Sanderson

Cody Sanderson (Navajo/Hopi/Pima/Nambe, b. 1964) creates metalwork forms that are experimental with unique designs. He likes to create "mechanical things that move, twist, and turn."[11] In part, these articulated works, usually executed in silver, distinguish his jewelry. For the 2006 Heard Museum Guild Indian Fair & Market, he made two tea infusers, one with a spring latch and the other attached to a cast leg and foot fashioned after his own and created to metaphorically resemble a ball and chain. He admits to adjusting the length of the toes on the foot.

Sanderson is a first-generation self-taught jeweler who learned by reading books, asking questions of other jewelers, and experimenting. In 1992, he took an initial jewelry class at a branch of the University of New Mexico in Gallup where he made a brass and nickel silver bracelet and a pair of silver earrings. He began making jewelry more se-

Cody Sanderson flask of silver, Lone Mountain turquoise, and 14k gold, 2005.

riously in 1999 and started by first buying tools with any extra money he made. By 2001, he had quit his job as a road salesman for M. M. Rogers, where he had worked for eight years, and was devoting his time to jewelry making. His first purchase after Indian Market in 2002 was a workbench, then shelves, and then lights. He set up his studio in the kitchen of the home he shared with his wife, Pilar—an accomplished fashion designer—and their four children.

Sanderson received verbal encouragement for jewelry making about two years before deciding to undertake it full time. He began by making money clips and quickly progressed to making rings and bracelets. But these are not your typical rings and bracelets. He has cast rings in the shape of a BMW tire, paying attention to the multiple spokes of the ring, and has made link bracelets out of silver sections cast from LEGOS, the plastic toys children use as building blocks. Even the less exotic conceptualized rings and bracelets have bold stamped designs on the reverse side.

Sanderson's work came to the attention of collectors when he participated in the Indian Market in Santa Fe in August 2002. Next, Sanderson participated in the 2003 Heard Museum Guild Indian Fair & Market. Two years later at the Heard Fair, the Heard purchased a silver flask with a Brazilian agate on the lid. Sanderson studied the pattern in the stone set into the flask lid and mirrored the pattern in silver on the underside of the lid and on the narrow sides of the flask.

The innovative silversmiths Kenneth Begay and Charles Loloma and the Scandinavian jeweler Georg Jensen have inspired Sanderson's work. He respects the fact that they paved the way for generations of jewelers through their innovative works. He also admires American Indian artists who, when met with an obstacle, look for innovative ways to respond to situations. He cites Hopi katsina doll carvers, who in the 1970s were restricted from using feathers of migratory birds and birds of prey, and responded by carving the details of the feathers and ultimately changing the art form. Just as Kenneth Begay and others moved away from the limitations set by art competitions, Sanderson advocates refusing to limit one's work to the restrictions of art shows that reward only traditional work and in-

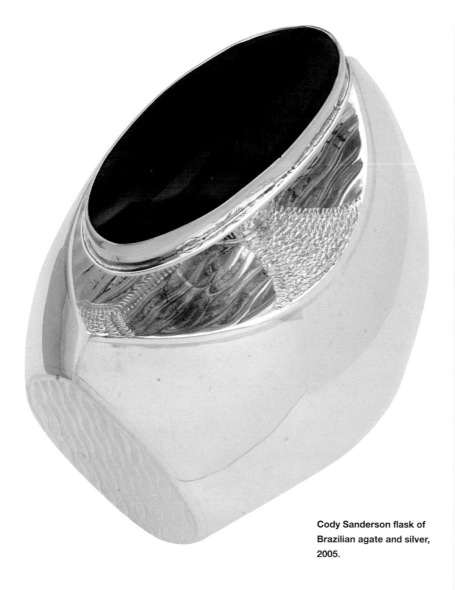

Cody Sanderson flask of Brazilian agate and silver, 2005.

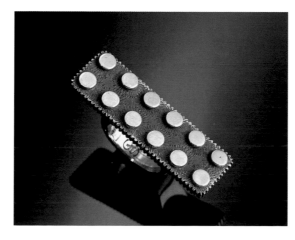

Cody Sanderson cast silver "legos" ring, 2006.

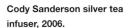

stead thinks jewelers should take advantage of non-traditional training when possible.

When he began making jewelry, Sanderson also began the practice of investing some percent of the proceeds from jewelry sales into tools and metal so that he could continue working. When he has purchased a tool, such as a belt sander or a new file, he likes to use it to justify the purchase.

When he set out to learn more about jewelry, Sanderson found that asking questions of other jewelers brought different reactions. Some were guarded with their answers, while others were open and generous with information. According to Sanderson, "Established artists have a sense of freedom to show me certain techniques or skills."[12] Vernon Haskie showed him how to polish stones. He took a casting class with David Gaussoin at the Poeh Center in Tesuque in 2002. After Gaussoin left the center in 2003, Sanderson began to teach there and found that teaching not only forced him to improve and grow but also provided a stimulus derived from working near other contemporary jewelers.

Although he is the first one in his family to make jewelry, Sanderson credits his mother, Anna Sanderson, for providing him with an interest in

Cody Sanderson "Ball and Chain" silver and 14k gold tea infuser, 2006.

Cody Sanderson silver tea infuser, 2006.

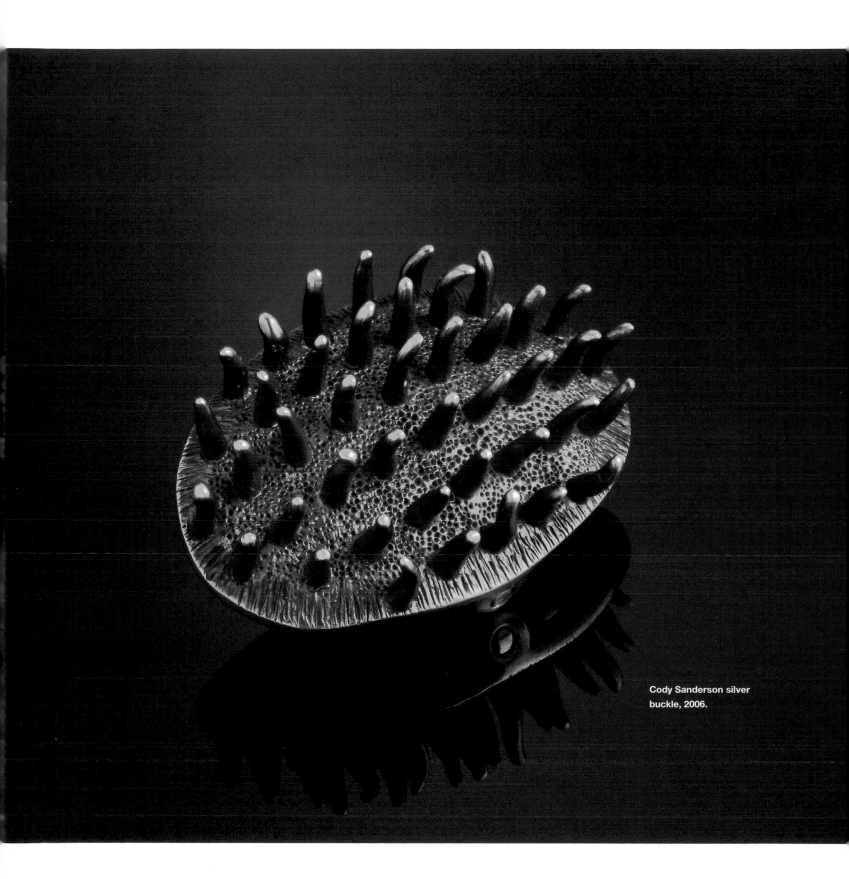

Cody Sanderson silver
buckle, 2006.

art. According to Sanderson, "We enjoy art. Mom loves it. We just never thought of doing it." He describes his jewelry and metalwork as "fun—not unfathomable—visually digestible."[13] Inspiration can come from a wide range of tangible concepts such as the LEGOS bracelet and the BMW tire ring, both derived from children's toys and Sanderson's recent years that have evolved around his role as father to his sons and daughter. Other life experiences have had an equal impact, and some have manifested themselves in creative works. When he began to make the ball and chain tea infuser, he remembered getting change for a pumpkin from a woman who kept her money in a hollowed artificial leg.

Since teaching the class at the Poeh Center, Sanderson has also experimented with casting techniques, at times combining tufa casting and cuttlefish bone casting. These he casts in sheets to be shaped into jewelry. One side has the design he carved into the tufa stone while the other has the softly swirled natural pattern of the cuttlefish bone.

Sanderson derives other concepts by experimenting with geometric shapes and, at times, adapting two-dimensional concepts to three-dimensional forms. His designs are bold and accentuate the silver. Deep repoussé lends dimension to a bracelet. Layers of spikes may adorn a buckle. At a glance the simplicity of the design may not reveal the time and effort made in the creation of the work. The spiked buckle was accomplished through lost wax casting, but texture was added by hammering the surface.

Sanderson begins working by sketching an initial idea in a sketchbook, on copper, or on leather. This allows him to visualize the finished design and experiment to determine how to make a concept a reality. Past conceptualities in copper or leather forms are stored in Sanderson's orderly and tool-filled studio.

Sanderson says of jewelry, "It is a labor of love. You have to enjoy what you're doing."[14]

Elizabeth Wallace

Elizabeth Wallace (Navajo/Washoe/Maidu, b. 1975) is accomplished in southwestern silversmithing techniques but also has studied *plique à jour*, one of the most difficult enameling techniques. Wallace is the first American Indian jeweler to use this technique. The subject matter of her work often reflects the natural world, and Wallace is also known for butterfly pins fashioned from silver with carved turquoise wings.

Wallace has been around jewelry all her life, although according to her, "I never picked up a torch [to make jewelry] until I was twenty years old."[15] Both her mother, Kathryn Morsea, and father, Alan Wallace, were jewelers, so Wallace grew up with an appreciation for the art form. Although she did not receive any formal instruction from her parents, Wallace recognized that she had an ability to work well with her hands. Her father had many books about jewelry, including *The Master Jewelers*, edited by Kenneth Snowman. Her review of those

Elizabeth Wallace cicada brooch of *plique á jour* enamel, silver, and carved mother of pearl, 2005.

Elizabeth Wallace pansy hair comb of plique-á-jour enamel, silver, and horn, 2003, and plique-á-jour enamel, silver, and shell cicada with articulated wings.

Opposite, top: Elizabeth Wallace oak leaf tiara of plique-á-jour enamel, turquoise, coral, and silver, 2006.

Opposite, bottom: Elizabeth Wallace turquoise and silver butterfly, 2004.

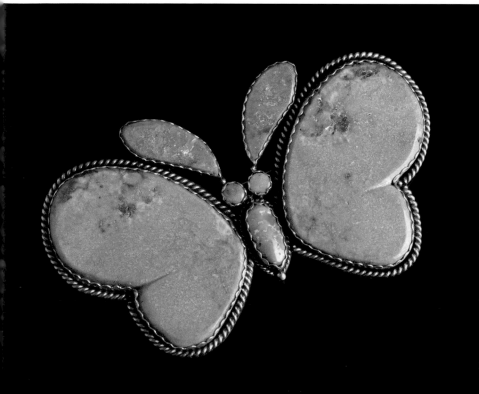

books when she was nineteen had a lasting impact on her understanding of and appreciation for jewelry. According to Wallace, "The word *fascinated* is not strong enough to describe my interest in the jewelry I saw pictures of in books, particularly the work of Renee Lalique."[16]

Wallace went to high school in Taos, New Mexico. After graduation she spent one year in California and then returned to New Mexico to settle in Santa Fe to work in the Indian art field. She took her first metalworking class that consisted of four consecutive sessions of four hours each over a period of a month at Santa Fe Community College. She also worked as a salesperson in the American Indian art antique market in Santa Fe, and during that time, she began repairing jewelry and other objects. As she gained some metalsmithing skills, she began to create her own jewelry. By

1996 she was making turquoise and silver twisted wire earrings and small dragonflies with wire wings, turquoise bodies, and paste (colored glass) eyes as well as butterflies out of silver wire.

In 1999, she made a series of small silver pins and earrings shaped like the historic Cochiti figures in the Wheelwright Museum's exhibit *Clay People* that were sold to the Wheelwright's Case Trading Post. They were fashioned from sheet silver, patterned after photographs of the historic figures, and some were so detailed as to include delineations of plants, jewelry, boots, and even toes. She made one necklace that had several of the silver figures attached for "Many Beautiful Colors." This was followed by a series of small, silver pottery-shaped pins that were made in conjunction with the exhibit of Dextra Quotskuyva's work, *Painted Perfection*, in 2001, again for the Case Trading Post.

Wallace's metalsmithing skills were broadened when she had the opportunity to work with silversmith Bob Bauver. She met Bauver at the antique shows where she also worked as a salesperson. In 2000, Bauver invited her to visit his workshop in New England in order to learn some different jewelry-making techniques. They were deciding what her first lesson should be, and Cindra Kline's book *Navajo Spoons* was on the kitchen table. Bauver and Wallace decided to cast silver spoons in local soapstone. They used Colonial silversmithing techniques, cast from silver ingots, and forged the spoons. Wallace was interested in experimenting with casting and found the process an intriguing one. The molten silver began to cool as soon as it touched the cold, sooted surface of the soapstone.

Wallace created a spoon shaped like a cowboy and Bauver made one in the shape of an Indian.

Wheelwright director Jonathan Batkin later saw Wallace's spoon and asked to include it in the museum's exhibit "A Stirring Story: Navajo and Pueblo Spoons." Wallace credits this as a turning point in her career. Although she had made numerous pins that were sold at the Wheelwright shop for two prior exhibits, she remained anonymous to most collectors and her minimalist hallmark gave no clues to her name. The inclusion of her spoon brought some name recognition to her at a time when she was beginning to develop her individualized jewelry style.

Wallace made three more trips to Bauver's studio over the next few years and learned tufa casting as well. Their common interest in Lalique's enamel works led Bauver to show her the enameling techniques of plique á jour, which he had learned through experimentation during college. Wallace says of plique á jour, "It is romantic, mysterious, and the effect is so beautiful. It can be as easy or as complex as you want to make it. To see Lalique's jewelry as a young artist meant so much."[17]

For a young jeweler, working with an experienced metalworker like Bauver also gave Wallace access to a great workshop outfitted with a range of tools. While at the workshop, Wallace and Bauver experimented with diverse materials, including animal horn. They tried different techniques, including boiling, to soften and shape the horn. One of Wallace's earliest accomplished works using plique á jour is a horn and enamel comb with a pansy design. Other creations using plique á jour are brooches in the shape of cicadas with carved shell or stone bodies and outstretched plique á jour enamel wings. One of these, purchased at the 47th Annual Heard Museum Guild Indian Fair & Market in 2005, has a carved mother of pearl body. Wallace carved only a few of shell. Finding that the particulates were so toxic during the carving process, she has resorted to carving stone bodies for this design.

For the 2006 Heard Fair, Wallace chose to make a plique á jour enamel and horn tiara in the shape of wild roses. She reflected on tribal nation beauty contests, a "vestige of European aristocracy," when contemplating the design. But she also thought of a recent Maidu Spring Dance in which she had recently participated, and it became one of the concepts behind the tiara. Wild irises and lilacs are woven to make wreaths for the dancers prior to the dance. The two concepts were juxtaposed to Wallace, who stated, "Taking indigenous plants and making them into head ornaments— adorning the head—is an archetypal event that happens across cultures." Wallace appreciated the contrast of the stark, cold properties of enameling in contrast to the soft, warm elements of the plants and was pleased with the results (in that some of the rose buds on the tiara look like real plants).

Wallace spent weeks planning the tiara, drawing designs on her living room wall, leaving it for a while, and then returning to examine and contemplate. According to Wallace, "With plique you have to plan every detail."[18] Wallace also likes the "magical" feel of drawing on the wall and leaves the drawings up for some time after the jewelry is created. The drawing of the tiara remained on the living room wall some five months after completion.

For the 2006 Indian Market in Santa Fe, Wallace created an oak leaf tiara. Wallace is also known for butterfly brooches fashioned from silver with carved turquoise wings as well as dragonflies made of turquoise. Like her peers, Wallace is interested in capturing movement in her work and has made a cicada with articulated wings.

Elizabeth Wallace turquoise and silver dragonfly with articulated tail, 2005.

Michael Kabotie steel gate for the Berlin Gallery, Heard Museum Shop, Phoenix, created in collaboration with Chris Duran, 2006.

Epilogue

No one can truly predict the future of contemporary jewelry, but exciting things continue to occur. In 2005, following several years of working on a mural project with the Museum of Northern Arizona in Flagstaff, Michael Kabotie created small-scale two-dimensional silver works inspired by the Awatovi murals. Although his bracelets had been based on mural designs, this was his attempt to treat jewelry as a two dimensional work of art rather than art to wear. The miniature silver murals were accompanied by large-scale drawings of the same design but in graphite and colored pencil. The miniature work and the large-scale drawing were side by side in his booth at the Heard Museum Guild Indian Fair & Market in 2005.

Kabotie took his interests a step further when, in 2006, he was asked by the Heard Museum staff to submit a mural drawing to be considered for a fence at one of the Heard's satellite locations. Although the project did not see fruition, Kabotie was asked to adapt the concept for a gate at the entrance of the newly constructed Berlin Gallery, a retail extension of the Heard Museum Shop. Kabotie worked collaboratively with sculptor Chris Duran to execute his concept, and the mural-based gate was installed in October 2006.

Other jewelry artists have collaborated as well. In 2002, Liz Wallace created a crown and hand-held mask of silver to accompany a figurative work created by ceramist and fashion design Virgil Ortiz. The silver work captures the essence of the painted curvilinear details on the face of the figure. The crown and mask provide an aura of mystique for the figure, and the combination of silver work and the painted face of the figure provided a slightly eerie result.

New materials have also been introduced in

jewelry work. Pat Pruitt began a business of designing and selling stainless steel body ornaments for piercings while a student at Southern Methodist University in Dallas, Texas. Pruitt continues his business but also developed a steel belt with casino chips submitted for the juried competition at the Heard Museum Guild Indian Fair & Market in 2006. Pruitt utilized the knowledge he gained while developing the pierce-work steel jewelry, combining it with the "traditional" concept of the concho belt. The belt, however, with its multicolored casino chips was anything but traditional. Using steel rather than silver completed the innovation. For the 2007 Heard Fair, Pruitt designed a spiked steel dog collar, which won the Conrad House Award for innovation. The bracelets and rings he creates have a delicacy of design in contrast to the powerful elements of steel.

Over the past fifty years, groundbreaking changes have occurred in American Indian jewelry. Those items that decades ago were removed from judging at competitions because they did not fit the categories are now considered to be classic jewelry designs. Each year, exciting new ideas are transformed into jewelry limitless in quality, color, and imagination.

Art based in tradition and art branching off of tradition have a history in American Indian art and in American Indian jewelry. Artists change and grow, and although change can create discomfort, it also is the stimulus for both discovery and discourse.

Elizabeth Wallace silver crown and mask created for a Virgil Ortiz ceramic and cloth figure, 2002.

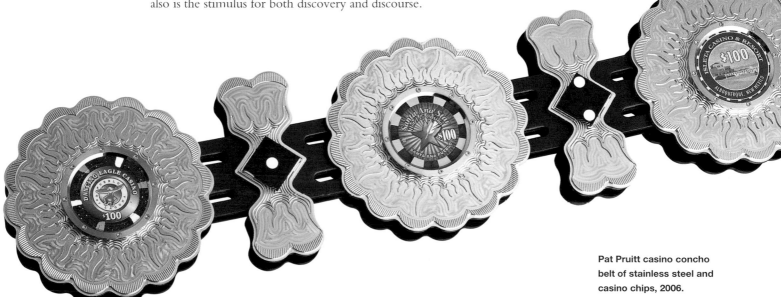

Pat Pruitt casino concho belt of stainless steel and casino chips, 2006.

Notes

Chapter 1

1   Charles Loloma's work has been extensively explored in the 2005 book by Martha H. Struever, *Loloma: Beauty Is His Name.*

2   See Pardue in *American Indian Art Magazine*, Summer 2005, 30, no. 3, 62–69.

3   Struever, *Loloma: Beauty Is His Name,* 4.

4   Ibid., 10–11.

5   Scottsdale Historic Preservation Office. Unpublished report.

6   Ibid.

7   Lloyd Kiva New and Fritz Scholder address at the Red Tuxedo, a fundraiser for the Native American Cultural Center, on March 1, 2001.

8   Struever, 15.

9   Clipped article, source and date unknown, Heard Museum Guild Scrapbook 1952–63, Heard Museum Library and Archives.

10 Clipped article with a handwritten date of February 1961. Heard Museum Guild Scrapbook 1961. Heard Museum Library and Archives.

11 *Arizona Republic*, March 23, 1962.

12 Gritton, "The Institute of American Indian Arts: A Convergence of Ideologies" in *Shared Visions,* 23.

13 Fritz Scholder address at the Red Tuxedo gala on March 1, 2001. Scholder reminisced of a time Charles Loloma suggested that the two men go to Scottsdale. They went to LuLu Belle's for lunch, out to see Philip Curtis in the desert and Paolo Soleri, and finished the day at the Pink Pony for drinks.

14 Scottsdale *Daily Progress*, January 7, 1964.

15 Montini, "Hopi Jeweler Tempts Buyers with Beauty," *Arizona Republic*, February 27, 1983.

16 New, "The Institue of American Indian Art," 15.

17 Hait, "Beads, Boots and Jaguars: The Artists as They See Themselves," 30.

Chapter 2

1   Adair, The Navajo and Pueblo Silversmiths, 18.

2   Ibid., 8.

3   Struever, in *Loloma: Beauty Is His Name*, established that Loloma was casting jewelry by 1946.

4   All biographical information about Preston Monongye has been reviewed by his son Jesse Monongya.

5   Larry Golsh, in discussion with the author, May 2006.

6   Ibid.

7   Ibid.

8   Steve LaRance, in discussion with the author, October 2006.

9   Pardue, The Cutting Edge, 34.

10 Ibid., 26.

11 "SWAIA Fellowships," 71.

12 Heil, "Navajo Artist Shows Her Mettle."

13 Adair, 30.

14 "SWAIA Fellowship Winners Announced," The Indian Trader, November 1995.

15 Debbie Silversmith, in discussion with the author, December 2006.

16 Adair, 24.

17 Adair, 37.

18 Norbert Peshlakai, unpublished artist statement provided to the author, 2007.

19 Pardue, The Cutting Edge, 41.

20 Coulson, "Artist Turned Down Rolls-Royce Offer" Casa Grande Tri Valley Dispatch, February 10–11, 1988.

21 Clark, "Jake Livingston IACA's 1988 'Artist of the Year.' "

22 Coulson, "Artist Turned Down Rolls-Royce Offer."

23 Darrell Jumbo, unpublished artist statement provided to the author, 2006.

24 Darrell Jumbo, in discussion with the author, October 2006.

25 Wright, Hopi Silver, 47–48.

26 "Qua'toqti," Oraibi, 4.

Chapter 3

1   For a complete discussion of their jewelry, see Diana F. Pardue, *Shared Images: The Innovative Jewelry of Yazzie Johnson and Gail Bird*, Santa Fe: Museum of New Mexico Press, 2007.

2   Adair, 148–49.

3   Slaney, 19.

4   For a complete discussion of Monongya's jewelry see Lois Dubin, *Jesse Monongya: Opal Bears and Lapis Skies*, Hudson Hill Press, 2002.

5   Indian Trader, November 1985, 7.

6   U.S. Department of the Interior, Indian Arts and Crafts Board, Southern Plains Indian Museum and Crafts Center, "Jewelry by Carolyn Bobelu, Pottery by Virginia Gutierrez, An Exhibition, October 14–November 30, 1984." Exhibit brochure from the Department of the Interior.

7   Vernon Haskie, in discussion with the author, October 31, 2006.

8   Pardue, *The Cutting Edge*, 38.

9   Slaney, 26–27. See Blue Gem, White Metal for a complete discussion of C. G. Wallace and Zuni jewelry from this time period.

10 Russ Whiting, "Shows Feature Work of Indian Artists," The Santa Fe New Mexican Pasa Tiempo, August 17–23, 1990.

11 Cheryl Yestewa, in discussion with the author, December 2006.

Chapter 4

1   McCoy, "Evolutionary Arts," *Southwest Profile: Arts and Travel Magazine*, 37–39.

2   Keri Ataumbi, unpublished artist statement provided to the author, 2006.

3   Jared Chavez, in discussion with the author, July 2006.

4   Ibid.

5   Jared Chavez, unpublished artist statement provided to the author, 2006.

6   Jared Chavez, in discussion with the author, July 2006.

7   Ibid.

8   Jared Chavez, unpublished artist statement provided to the author, 2006.

9   Maria Samora, unpublished artist statement provided to the author, October 2006.

10 Ibid.

11 Cody Sanderson, in discussion with the author, July 2006.

12 Ibid.

13 Ibid.

14 Ibid.

15 Liz Wallace, in discussion with the author, July 2006.

16 Ibid.

17 Ibid.

18 Ibid.

Photo Credits

Faust, Bill: page 123 (bottom), page 124 (top)

Gandert, Miguel: page 141 (bottom), page 146, page 152 (top), page 156. page, 159 (top), page 163 (top), page 166 (left), page 170, page 171 (top), page 174

Golsh, Larry: page 32, page 33 (top), page 83 (top)

Georges, Lauren: page 49 (bottom), page 80 (top), page 86, page 97 (both)

Haines, Murrae: page 96 (bottom)

Howard, Kathleen: page 58 (bottom)

Karshis, Phil: page 188

Lizard Light Productions: page 36 (bottom), page 50 (lower left), page 68 (left), page 108 (top), page 111 (lower right)

Nohl, Mark: page 129, page 147, page 172, page 173 (top)

Jewelry Collection Credits

All jewelry is from private collections unless noted.

Heard Museum Collection: pages 13 (bottom), 14, 15, 16 (bottom), 18, 19, 23 (middle and bottom), 25, 26, 29, 30 (Fred Fine Arts Collection at the Heard), 31, 35 (left), 36, 37 (left), 44, 45, 46, 47 (left), 49 (left), 50 (bottom), 56, 57, 59 (left), 64 (top), 65, 67 (bottom), 72, 73, 76 (bottom), 79 (right), 80 (bottom), 85, 88 (left), 89, 90 (left), 91, 92, 93 (top), 99, 103 (left), 104, 107, 110, 111 (top), 115, 116 (left), 117, 124 (bottom), 125, 126, 130, 131, 140, 144, 162 (bottom), 166, 167 (top), 171, 173 (bottom), and 177 (top).

Norman L. Sandfield Collection at the Heard Museum: pages 50 (right), 54 (left), 64 (bottom), 67 (top), 83 (bottom), 84 (bottom), and 149.

Heard Museum Guild Indian Fair & Market: pages 71 (top), 74, 75, 93 (bottom), 108 (left), 112, 116 (bottom), 118 (bottom), 123 (top), and 177 (bottom).

Heard Museum Shop: pages 4, 33 (bottom), 35 (bottom), 37 (bottom), 38 (left), 39, 40, 41 (top), 42, 49 (right), 50 (left), 52, 59 (right), 60, 61, 69 (top), 70 (bottom), 71 (bottom), 77, 79 (left), 82 (bottom), 87, 90 (right), 103 (right), 105, 106 (left), 111 (bottom), 116 (top right), 119 (bottom), 120 (left), 127 (top), 128 (bottom), 132 (top), 135, 152, 153 (bottom), and 167 (bottom).

Albuquerque International Sunport and 1% for the Public Arts Program: page 134.

American Indian Art Magazine: page 175.

JoAnn and Robert Balzer: page 100.

HMC Collection: page 102 (top).

Diana Douglass Collection: page 136.

Andy Eisenberg Collection: pages 48, 55, 108 (right), 141, 144, 154, 156, 157, 160 (bottom), 161, 162 (top), 164, and 165.

Bill Faust Gallery: 123 (bottom) and 124 (top).

Dr. and Mrs. Halbert F. Gates Collection: pages 13 (top), 16 (top), and 24.

Jan Hendler Collection: pages 155, 157 (top), and 158.

Anne Kern Collection: page 132 (bottom).

Kersting Collection: pages 113, 118 (top), and 119 (top).

J. L. Pete and Sara Morgan Collection: page 160 (top).

Private Collection, Dallas: pages 100 and 114.

Gary, Brenda and Harrison Ruttenberg Collection: page 95.

Fred and Helen Spielman Collection: pages 49 (bottom), 80 (top), 86, and 97.

Martha H. Struever Collection: page 100.

Bibliography

Adair, John. *Navajo and Pueblo Silversmiths.* Norman: University of Oklahoma Press, 1944. *Arizona Republic,* March 23, 1962.

Bird, Allison. *Heart of the Dragonfly: The Historical Development of the Cross Necklaces of the Pueblo and Navajo Peoples.* Albuquerque: Avanyu Publishing, 1992.

Bonnell, Mary. "Hopi Silversmith." *The Arizona Republic,* October 13, 1974.

Clark, Jackson. "Jake Livingston IACA's 1988 'Artist of the Year.'" *The Indian Trader,* November 1987.

Coulson, Linda. "Artist Turned Down Rolls-Royce Offer." *Casa Grande Tri Valley Dispatch,* February 10–11, 1988.

Dubin, Lois Sherr. *Jesse Monongya: Opal Bears and Lapis Skies.* New York: Hudson Hills Press, 2002.

Gritton, Joy. "The Institute of American Indian Arts: A Convergence of Ideologies." *Shared Visions,* Phoenix: Heard Museum, 1991.

Hait, Pam. "Beads, Boots and Jaguars: The Artists as They See Themselves." *Arizona Highways,* 55, no. 4 (1979): 30–32.

Heard Museum Guild Scrapbooks 1952–1963, Heard Museum Library and Archives.

Heard Museum Library and Archives Artist Files.

Heil, Diana. "Navajo Artist Shows Her Mettle." *The Daily Times.* Farmington, New Mexico, June 23, 1999.

The Independent Gallup. "Art Show Features Metalwork." June 3, 1999.

Indian Trader. "IACA's Top Artists: Carolyn Bobelu." 16, no. 10 (November 1985): 7.

Indian Trader. "SWAIA Fellowship Winners Announced." 26, no. 11 (November 1995): 17.

Kelly, Tim. "Journey to a Far Country: Presenting the Art Work of Phillip C. Curtis of Scottsdale." *Arizona Highways,* 39, no. 11 (1963): 14–37.

Loscher, Tricia. "Mid-Century Modern: Native American Art in Scottsdale," an exhibit at the Heard Museum North, January 28–August 13, 2006.

McCoy, Ron. "Evolutionary Arts." *Southwest Profile: Arts and Travel Magazine,* March/April 1986, 37–39.

McGough, Mellen. "Women Who Rock." *Indian Market Magazine,* August 2004, 192–93.

Monthan, Guy and Doris. *Art and Indian Individualists.* Flagstaff: Northland Press, 1975.

Montini, E. J. "Hopi Jeweler Tempts Buyers with Beauty." *The Arizona Republic,* February 27, 1983.

New, Lloyd. "The Institute of American Indian Art," *Arizona Highways,* 48, no. 1 (1972): 12–15.

Pallack, Becky. "Carving His Place in the Art World." *Arizona Daily Sun,* June 10, 2001.

Pardue, Diana F. *The Cutting Edge: Contemporary Native American Jewelry and Metalwork.* Phoenix: Heard Museum, 1997.

Pardue, Diana F. "Expect the Unexpected: Native American Jewelry and Beadwork." *Ornament,* 25, no. 3 (2002): 42–45.

Pardue, Diana F. "Native American Silversmiths in the Southwest." *American Indian Art Magazine,* 30, no. 3 (2005): 62–69.

Pardue, Diana F. *Shared Images: The Innovative Jewelry of Yazzie Johnson and Gail Bird.* Santa Fe: Museum of New Mexico Press, 2007.

Pardue, Diana F. "Majestic Opal." *Frontdoors,* February 2006, 39.

Qua'toqti, Oraibi, Arizona. "Distinguished Second Mesa Silversmith." January 24, 1980, 4.

Robinson, Andrea. "Shawn Bluejacket: Life Is About Beauty." *Ornament.* 25, no. 4 (2002): 58–61.

Scholder, Fritz. Address at the Red Tuxedo, A Fundraiser for the Native American Cultural Center, March 1, 2001.

Scottsdale Daily Progress, January 7, 1964.

Slaney, Deborah. *Blue Gem, White Metal: Carvings and Jewelry from the C. G. Wallace Collection.* Phoenix: Heard Museum, 1998.

Struever, Martha H. *Loloma: Beauty Is His Name.* Santa Fe: Wheelwright Museum of the American Indian, 2005.

"SWAIA Fellowships," *Indian Market Magazine,* 1998, 71.

U.S. Department of the Interior, Indian Arts and Crafts Board, Southern Plains Indian Museum and Crafts Center. "Jewelry by Carolyn Bobelu, Pottery by Virginia Gutierrez, an Exhibition. October 14–November 30, 1984." Exhibit brochure.

Whiting, Russ. "Shows Feature Work of Indian Artists." *The Santa Fe New Mexican Pasa Tiempo,* August 17–23, 1990.

Wright, Margaret. *Hopi Silver.* Flagstaff: Northland Press, 1972.

Index

acid etching, 12, 154
Adair, John, 99, 115, 139
agates, 26, 99, 167
Aguilar, Benny, 130
Ah-Be-Hill, Jeri, 141
amber, 14, 128, 145
American Indian Art Magazine, 22
American Indian Artists II (PBS series), 36
appliqué technique, 43, 68, 85–88
Arcosanti, Arizona, 32
Arizona Biltmore (Phoenix), 11
Arizona Craftsman Center, 12–13
Arizona Highways: Jacka as photographer for, 42–43; topics of back issues, 18, 20, 22, 24, 38; Raymond Yazzie and, 119
Art and Indian Individualists (Monthan), 36
Ataumbi, Keri, **140–144,** 141–145
Awatovi murals, 89

Batkin, Jonathan, 174
Bauver, Bob, 174
beads, 57, 63, 130–137
Beck, Victor, **136,** 137
Bedonie, Ron, 74, **77**
Begay, Harvey, 11, **35,** 36–38
Begay, Johnnie Mike, 43
Begay, Kenneth: design background, 11–12, 20, **21;** Little and, 43; metalwork, 29, 43; Sanderson and, 167; Silversmith and, 63; stone patterning, **99;** Tso and, 52
Bird, Charlie, 114, **114**
Bird, Gail: bead necklaces and, 137; design background, 11, 25–26, 96; jewelry designs, **40, 94–96,** 100–102, 132–135; stone patterning and, 99–100
Bird, Lorencita, 59
Bird-Romero, Allison, 57
Bird-Romero, Mike: designs by, **59, 71, 105–106;** doming and, 57–63; stone patterning and, 99
Bluejacket, Shawn, 99–102, **103–104**
Bobelu, Carolyn, **117,** 119
Bonnell, John, 12, 43
Bonnell, Jon, 43
Boone, Lena, 126
Branson, Oscar, 110
brass: Johnson's use of, 99; King's use of, 52; raising process, 43; Sanderson's use of, 166; Tenorio's use of, 96

Cain, H. Thomas, 16
Caldwell, Leona, 12
casting, 30–43. *See also* lost wax casting; tufa casting

Casuse, Fritz, **54–55,** 56
channelwork, 115, 119
charcoal, casting technique with, 34
Charlie, Ric, **36–38,** 38–40
charoite, 11, 25
Chavez, Cynthia, 146
Chavez, Jared, 146–149, **146–151**
Chavez, Richard: design background, 11, 25, 109, 146; jewelry designs, **107, 122**
Chee, Mark, 59
Clark, Carl and Irene, **121,** 123–124
Coffey, Karita, 152
Coochwytewa, Victor, 89, **89**
copper: early objects made of, 7; Gaussoin's use of, 152; Lee's use of, 85; raising technique, 43; Sanderson's use of, 170
coral: bead jewelry and, 130, **130;** Begay's use of, 38; Loloma's use of, **13, 14, 15, 19;** Monongye's use of, 30
Coulter, Lane, 56, 100
Cowboy Slim, **66,** 66–67
Craft Center (Scottsdale), 12
Crazy Horse, Cippy, **62,** 71–72, **72**
Croft, Anna Fullen, 11
Cummings, Edison: fabrication and, **41,** 43–52, **45–46;** repoussé and, 73—74, **74–76;** stone inlay and, **120–121,** 123
Curtis, Jennifer, **61,** 63
Curtis, Phillip, 12
Curtis, Thomas, Sr., 63
Custen, Calvin, 146
cuttlefish bone casting: Gaussoin's use of, 152; Golsh's use of, 26, 34–35; Sanderson's use of, 170

Da, Tony, 20, **21,** 22
Dawahoya, Bernard, 89–91
Denipah, Marilyn, 40
Dewey Gallery (Santa Fe), 25–26, 56
DeYoung, Connie, 152
Deyuse, Leekya, 125, **125**
diamonds: Ataumbi's use of, 145; Harvey Begay's use of, 38; Golsh's use of, 36; Little's use of, 43; Montongya's use of, 118; Samora's use of, 164; setting, 29, 128; Supplee's use of, 128
doming technique, **56,** 57–63
Dunn, Dorothy, 20
Duran, Antonio, 59
Duran, Chris, 176

Edaakie, Dennis, 71
Eight Northern Indian Pueblos Council, 56
enameling techniques, 171
Eustace, Benjamin, 55
Eustace, Christina, **50–51,** 55–56, **129**
Eustace, Felicita, 55

fabrication, metalwork, 43–56, 159
Faks, James (Sinopah): design background, 78–79, 128; designs by, **69–70, 79, 128**
Fashion Institute of Technology (FIT), 159

fetish necklaces, 125, **126**
fossilized ivory, **19,** 25
Foutz, John, 68
Fred Harvey hotels, 30

Gallery 10 (Scottsdale), 56
Gallup Inter-Tribal Ceremonial: Monongye and, 20, 30–31; Norbert Peshlakai and, 68; Shorty and, 57; Tenorio and, 96; Raymond Yazzie and, 119
Gasper, Dinah, 126
Gaussoin, Connie: design background, 56, 152, 156; designs by, **55**
Gaussoin, David: design background, 56, 152–154, 156; designs by, **152–155;** Sanderson and, 168
Gaussoin, Tazbah, 154
Gaussoin, Wayne, 56, 156, **156–158**
Gchachu, Terry, 159
gold: Harvey Begay's use of, 38; casting technique, 30; Harris's use of, 53; Michael Kabotie's use of, 89; Loloma's use of, 30; Monongye's use of, 31; Samora's use of, 164
Golden Gate International Exposition, 12
Golsh, Larry: awards for, 35; design background, 11, 22, 26; jewelry designs, **32–34, 83;** Loloma and, 32; metalwork and, 31–36
Goo, Ben, 32
Goodluck, Hosteen, **85**
Gorman, R. C., 20
granulation, 78, 107
Greeves, Teri, 141

Haloo, Jacob, Sr., 71
Hardin, Helen, 20, 22
Harris, Cheyenne, **46–48,** 52–53
Haskie, Vernon, **118,** 119–122, 168
Heard, Maie Bartlett, 65
Heard Museum: art competitions, 12, 20, **21;** Cummings and, 73; Faks and, 79; David Gaussoin and, 154; Jumbo and, 81; Loloma and, 16–17, **17,** 20; Dylan Poblano and, 159
Heard Museum Guild Arts and Crafts Exhibit: competitions at, 12; Golsh and, 35; judges' photo, 21; Little and, 43; Monongye and, 30
Heard Museum Guild Indian Fair & Market: Ataumbi and, 143, 145; Charlie and, **36;** Cummings and, 47; Haskie and, **118,** 122; Michael Kabotie and, 176; Lee and, **86;** Loloma and, 16–17; Angie Owen and, **111;** Pruitt and, 177; Charlene Reano and, 112; repoussé work, 73; Sanderson and, 166–167; Tenorio and, **93,** 96; Elizabeth Wallace and, 175; Raymond Yazzie and, **116,** 119
Heard Museum Shop, 17, 35, 176
Heart of the Dragonfly (Bird-Romero), 57
Holbrook, Millard, 53
Hopi Guild, 30
Houser, Allan: design background, 17, 20, **21;** Loco and, 81
Hubbell, John Lorenzo, 30
Hubbell, Roman, 30

Indian Arts and Crafts Association, 71, **117**
Indian Market, Santa Fe: Ataumbi and, 145; Bird and, 99; Jared Chavez and, 146–149; Cummings and, 47; Connie Gaussoin and, 56; David Guassoin and, 154; Wayne Gaussoin and, 156; Yazzie Johnson and, 99; Jumbo and, 81; Navaasya and, 55; Natasha Peshlakai and, 81; Daniel Reeves and, 68; Sanderson and, 167; Elizabeth Wallace and, 175
Indian Tree Gallery (Chicago), 25
inlay designs: Loloma's use of, 16, 18, **19**, 23–24, 25, **25**, 29; stone patterning, 115–124
Institute of American Indian Arts (IAIA): Ataumbi and, 145; Casuse and, 56; Cummings and, 43; Denipah and, 40; Connie Gaussoin and, 56; David Guassoin and, 152, 154; Wayne Gaussoin and, 156; King and, 53; LaRance and, 40; Loloma and, 18; Lovato and, 40; Maktima and, 109; Metoxen and, 56; New and, **16**, 17; Tenorio and, 96
ironwood: Kenneth Begay's use of, 29; Cummings' use of, 47, 123; White Hogan and, 12, 43

Jacka, Jerry, 25, 43
Jacka, Lois, 25
jasper, 26, 99
Jensen, Georg, 167
jet: alternatives for, 110; bead jewelry and, 130; historical use of, 12; King's use of, 53; Maktima's use of, 109; stone patterning and, 99
Johnson, Maryon, 12
Johnson, Yazzie: bead necklaces and, 137; design background, 11, 25–26, 96; jewelry designs, **40, 94–96, 100–102, 132–135**; stone patterning and, 99–100
Jumbo, Darrell, **79–80,** 79–81, **84**

Kabotie, Fred: design background, 12, 20, 89; jewelry design, **21**
Kabotie, Michael (Lomawywesa): design background, 20, 89; designs by, **90, 176**; mural project, 176
katsina dolls: *Arizona Highways* article on, 18; Dawahoya and, 89; LaRance and, 40; Sanderson and, 167; Susunkewa and, 32; Carroll Yestewa and, 137
Kee, Allan, 12, 43
Kee, George, 12, 43
Kee, Ivan, 43
King, Monica, **49,** 53
Kirk, Mike, 66
Kiva Craft Center, 14, 32
Klein, Calvin, 20
Kline, Cindra, 174
KOY radio station, 91

Lalique, Renee, 173–174
lapidary work: Bluejacket and, 100; Bobelu and, 119; Eustace and, 56; Golsh and, 36; Monongye and, 31; silver foundations for, 115; three-dimensional work, 125

lapis lazuli: Loloma and, 11, **19**, 25; Monongya and, 115
LaRance, Steve, **38,** 40
Lauren, Ralph, 7, 20
Lee, Clarence, **85,** 85–87, **86**
Lee, Russell, 85, **86**
Leek, John Gordon, **115**
Leki, Edna, 125–126, **126**
Lister, Ernie, 57
Little, James, 11, **42,** 43
liver of sulphur, 38
Livingston, Jake, 70–71, **71**
Loco, Jan, 78, 81, **82**
Loloma, Charles: Ataumbi and, 141; Beck and, 137; Bird and, 99–100; Charlie and, 38; Cummings and, 123; design background, 11–26; designs by, **13–19, 21–27, 126**; Golsh and, 32; honors/awards, 130; inlay designs, 96, 115, 126; Yazzie Johnson and, 99–100; metalwork, 29–30; Nequatewa and, 122; photo of, **17**; Sanderson and, 167
Loloma, Otellie, 12–13, 17
Lomahaftewa, Linda, 152
Lomay, Lewis, 22
Lomayestewa, Mark, 89
Lomayestewa, McBride, 89
lost wax casting: Harvey Begay's use of, 38; Eustace's use of, 56; Little's use of, 43; Loloma's use of, 17–18, **18**; Dylan Poblano and, 159
Lovato, Anthony, **39,** 40–43, 130
Lovato, Charles, **131**
Lovato, Julian, 59
Lovato, Mary, 40
Lovato, Sedelio F., 40

Maktima, Duane: Bluejacket and, 100; designs by, **96–97**; fabrication and, 53–54; David Gaussoin and, 154; stone patterning and, 107–109
malachite, 11, 25
Mansfield, Jayne, 20
Martinez, Maria, 22
The Master Jewelers (Wallace), 171
McArthur, Albert Chase, 11
McHorse, Joel, 56
metalwork: appliqué, 43, 85–88; Ataumbi and, 145; casting, 30–43; doming, 57–63; fabrication, 43–56; overlay, 88–97; Poblano and, 162; repoussé, 43, 73–77; stamp work, 43, 64–72; stone patterning and, 98–109; texturing metal, 78–84; Wallace and, 174
Metoxen, Linda Lou, **54,** 56
Michaels, Patricia, 154
Mike, Johnnie, 12
Mission baskets, 36
Momaday, Al, 20, **21**
Monongya, Jesse: design background, 11, 31, 115–118; jewelry design, **31, 116, 124**
Monongye, David, 30
Monongye, Preston: awards, 30–31; Charlie and, 38; design background, 11, 20, 22; jewelry design, **30**; metalwork, 29, 30; Monongya and, 115

Monthan, Guy and Doris, 36
Montoya, Geronima, 20
Monument Valley: Charlie and, 37–38, 40; Clarence Lee and, 87; Monongya and, 118
Morez, Mary, 20
Morsea, Kathryn, 171
mosaic on shell or wood, 110–114, 124
mother of pearl, 112, 175
Motto, Chien, 163
Mullan, Read, 22
Museum of Man (San Diego), 156
Museum of Northern Arizona: Michael Kabotie and, 176; Little and, 43; Loloma and, **16**; Anthony Lovato and, 40; Maktima and, 107; Monongye and, 31; silver overlay and, 88–89

Nampeyo (potter), 91
National Museum of the American Indian, 146–147
Navaasya, Phil, **52,** 54–55
Navajo and Pueblo Silversmiths (Adair), 99, 139
Navajo Spoons (Kline), 174
needlepoint, 119
Nequatewa, Verma: design background, 115, 122–123; designs by, **119, 123–124**
New, Betty, 31–32
New, Lloyd Kiva: design background, 12–13, 16–18, 26; Golsh and, 31–32
New Mexico Magazine, 18, 20, 22
New Mexico State Fair, 31
Nez, Gibson, 70, **70**
Nichols, Mareen, 16

Ohl, Lovena: design background, 17; Golsh and, 35–36; Little and, 43; Supplee and, 128
O'Leary, Dennis, 20
olive shells, 96
opals, 100–102, 109, 114
Oreland Joe, 56
Ortiz, Virgil, 154, 176, **177**
overlay technique, 26, 88–97
Owen, Angie, 110–112, **111,** 114
Owen, Don, 114

Panteah, Martin, 53
Panteah, Myron, **49,** 53, 109
Panteah, Sybil, 53
Parker, Jim, 35
Parker, Stanley, 68
Partha, Nyoman, 141–143
Patania, Frank, 130
pearls: Ataumbi and, 145; Bird and, 137; Johnson and, 36; Loloma and, 17
Penland School of Craft, 143
Peshlakai, Aaron, 81
Peshlakai, Linda, 66–67, 81
Peshlakai, Natasha, 81–82, **83–84**
Peshlakai, Norbert: children of, 81–82; design background, 7, 11, 25–26; designs of, **64, 67–68**; fabrication, 54; Jumbo and, 79, 81; photo of, **68**; stamp work, 66–68; texturing the metal, 78

petit point, 55

petroglyphs: Jumbo and, 81; Michael Kabotie and, 89; LaRance and, 40; Loco and, 81; Kee Yazzie, Jr. and, 54

Phoenix Indian Hospital, 31

Phoenix Indian School, 12, 31

Pink Pony pub, 12

pink spinel, 14

plique à jour, 171, 174

Poblano, Dylan, 154, 159–162, **159–162**

Poblano, Jovana, 106

Poblano, Leo, 102, 125, 159

Poblano, Veronica, 102–107, **106**, 159

Poeh Arts Center: Casuse and, 56; David Gaussoin and, 154; Sanderson and, 168, 170

Poirier, Phil, 163

Polelonema, Walter, 89

Price, Vincent, 17

Pruitt, Pat, 177, **177**

Public Broadcasting Consortium series, 36

Pueblo Five Institute: David Gaussoin and, 154; Maktima and, 109; Panteah and, 53; Kee Yazzie, Jr. and, 54

Pueblo Opera Program, 154

Quintana, Evelyn, 59

Quintana, Joe H., 71

Quintana, Terecita, 71

Qumayintewa, Alde, 93

Quotskuyva, Dextra, 174

raising technique, 43

Randall, Tony, 20

Reano, Charlene Sanchez, **112–113**, 112–114

Reano, Clara, 110, 112

Reano, Frank, 112

Reano, Isidro, 110

Reano, Joe B., 130, **131**

Reano, Joe I., 110, 112

Reano, Terry, 130, **131**

Reeves, Daniel "Sunshine," **65**, 68–70

Reeves, David, 74

Reeves, Gary, 68, 74, **77**

Reeves, Leroy, 74

repoussé: Eustace and, 56; overview, 43, 73–77; Sanderson and, 170

reticulation, 78

Robinson, Morris, **44**

Rockefeller Foundation, 17, 20

rocker engraving, 43, 65

Rogers, M. M., 167

Roosevelt, Eleanor, 13

rosarita, 109

Ross, Jack, Mrs., 17

Saks Fifth Avenue, 7, 22

Sakyesva, Harry, 91

Samora, Frank, 163

Samora, Maria, 163–164, **163–165**

San Marcos Resort, 11

Sanderson, Cody, 166–170, **166–170**

Sandfield, Norman, 148

Sandoval, Ramoncita, 22

Santa Fe Indian School, 20

Saufkie, Paul, **88**, 88–89

Scholder, Fritz, 13, 17, 20

School for American Craftsmen (Alfred University), 12

Scott, Ray, 53

Scottsdale, artists associated with, 11–13, 17, 36

Scottsdale Progress, 16

Second Mesa Day School, 12

Sekaquaptewa, Wayne, 91, 93

Sekayumptewa, Wally, 89

shells: acid etching, 12; beads from, 130; carvings in, 125–129; Maktima's use of, 109; Monongye's use of, 30; mosaic on, 110–114

Shorty, Perry, 57, **58**, 88, **88**

Sikyakti ruins, 89, 91

silver: appliqué technique, 85; casting technique, 30; doming, 57; flatware in, 52–53; floral patterns in, 56; inlay patterns in, 16, 18, **19, 23–25**; lapidary work and, 115; liver of sulphur in, 38; lost wax casting, 17–18, **18**; overlay technique on, 26, 88; rocker engraving, 43; from sheet silver, 14; silversmithing techniques, 32; stamping, 65; texturing the metal, 78; tufa casting, 13, **18, 22**; turquoise and, 99; Wallace and, 174

Silversmith, Debbie, **59–60**, 63

Skaggs, H. Fred, 13

Skeet, Roger, **99**

Smith, Anna Fullen, 11

Snowman, Kenneth, 171

Soleri, Paolo, 32–35

Southwestern Association of American Indian Arts (SWAIA): Jumbo and, 81; Panteah and, 53; Shorty and, 57; Raymond Yazzie and, 119

squash blossom jewelry, 20, 31, 70

stained glass, 56

stamp work: Jared Chavez and, 147; David Gaussoin and, 152; overview, 43, 64–72; Panteah and, 53; Norbert Peshlakai and, 66–68, 82

Stanton, John D., 12–13

steel: Cummings' use of, 52; David Gaussoin's use of, 152–154; King's use of, 53; Norbert Peshlakai's use of, 66; Pruitt's use of, 177

stone patterning: bead necklaces, 130–137; carvings in stone and shell, 125–129; metal and stonework, 98–109; mosaic on shell or wood, 110–114; stone inlay, 115–124

Storer, Sanford, 68, **72**

Streuver, Martha (Hopkins), 25, **58**

Supplee, Charles: design background, 11, 42, 126–128; designs by, **121, 127–128**

Supplee, Don, **35**, 38

Susunkewa, Manfred, 32

Takala, Jason, 93, **97**

Taliesin West, 12

Tanner, Joe, 118

Taos Institute of Art, 163

Tarzan and the Leopard Woman (film), 17

Taylor, Carl, 87

Taylor, Robert, 87, **87**

Tenorio, Roderick, **93**, 96

texturing metal, 53, 78–84

Thunderbird Shop, 130

Toledo, Jose Rey, 130

Touraine, Pierre, 36, 93, 128

tourmaline, 14

Tsinajinnie, Andrew, 17

Tso, Roberta Multine, 52

Tsosie, Carol, 22

Tsosie, Nelson, 56

tufa casting: Begay's use of, 38, 63; Casuse's use of, 56; Charlie's use of, 38, 40; Connie Gaussoin's use of, 56; David Gaussoin's use of, 152; Golsh's use of, **32–33**; LaRance's use of, 40; Loloma's use of, 11, 13, 16, **17, 22**; Anthony Lovato and, 40, 43; Monongya's use of, **31**; Monument Valley design, 40; overview, 11, 30; Silversmith's use of, 63

turquoise: *Arizona Highways* issue on, 22; bead jewelry and, 130; Cummings' use of, 73–74; Curtis' use of, 63; Eustace's use of, 55; fetish necklaces, 125; Golsh's use of, 36; historical use of, 12; in inlaid patterns, 16, 18, **19**; Loloma's use of, 20, 25; Monongye's use of, 30; mosaic patterns of, 110; silver and, 99

underlay technique, 26, 96, 100

University of New Mexico: Ataumbi and, 145; Eustace and, 56; Gaussoin and, 152; Sanderson and, 166

Up With People, 56

Wallace, Alan, 171

Wallace, C. G., 115, 125

Wallace, Elizabeth, **171–175**, 171–176, **177**

Weahkee, Anderson, 126

Weahkee, Teddy, 125–126

Westword Ho (Phoenix), 11

Wheelright Museum, 130, 174

White Hogan (Scottsdale), 12, 36–37, 43

Wigwam (Litchfield), 11

Will Success Spoil Rock Hunter? (film), 20

wood: casting technique with, 34; mosaic on, 110–114

woodblock printmaking, 147

Works Progress Administration, 12

Wright, Frank Lloyd, 11–12

Yazzie, Jimmy, 53

Yazzie, Kee, Jr., **50**, 53–54, 109

Yazzie, Lee: design background, 22, 31; stone inlay and, 116, 118

Yazzie, Mary, 22

Yazzie, Raymond, **116**, 118–119, **123**

Yei figures, 20

Yestewa, Carroll, 137

Yestewa, Cheryl, **132**, 137

Yoyokie, Gary and Elsie, **92**, 93–96